MW01124205

FOUNDATIONS
of the
FAITH

a capstone church study guide
JON DUGDALE

ISBN-13:9780615864730

DEDICATION

This Study Guide is dedicated to the Lord Jesus Christ -
Who first loved me and saved me -
Whose mercies toward me are new every morning.

I also acknowledge the love and support of Barb,
my wife of 41 years - the one whose life and Christian witness
when we met - helped draw me to seek the Lord
and come to know Him when I was lost.

CONTENTS

Chapter	Title	Page
-	Foreword	7
-	Introduction	9
1	The Bible is the Word of the Living God.........................	11
2	God is the Creator and Sustainer of Everything...............	27
3	God the Father, the Son, and the Holy Spirit....................	38
4	Jesus is Savior, Lord, and Christ	54
5	The Holy Spirit is sent by Jesus and the Father	75
6	The Nine Gifts of the Holy Spirit	87
7	Share the Good News of the Kingdom	101
8	Jesus Christ is Coming Again	108
9	Lessons from the School of Prayer	122
10	Stewardship is Faith's Response to God	140
-	Index - Chapter Subheadings and Appendices	152

The appendix at the end of each chapter provides additional study material to help readers to strengthen the foundations of their faith in the Lord Jesus Christ.

FOREWORD

If the foundations are destroyed, what can the righteous do?"
(Psalm 11:3)

The foundation is the most important part of any building. If it is not built correctly, everything built on top of it will be off. At the beginning, things may not look that bad. But, as more and more is built on top of what already exists, the fault in the foundation becomes more pronounced.

Successful buildings start with a foundation built true to form. It is the same with your spiritual life. Foundations of the Faith will make sure that your spiritual foundation has been put down true to form. True to what form? The form we call the Word of God! If deception or error exists in our understanding of the foundations of the faith, then it becomes easier to be deceived regarding future spiritual revelations.

Since error already exists in our understanding of God and His revelation then all we are exposed to in the future regarding Christ's involvement in the world and our personal lives will be filtered through that error. Many feel that they don't have a need for or the time to study the foundations. But like a football player who lacks understanding of the fundamentals of the game that he plays, that lack of knowledge will soon show up in his performance.

Take the time to lay the proper foundation in your spiritual life! The evidence of your attention to detail will be noticed in all God calls you to do for the rest of your life!

Jesus said in Luke 6:47-48: *"Whoever comes to Me, and hears My sayings and does them, I will show you whom he is like: He is like a man building a house, who dug deep and laid the foundation on the rock. And when the flood arose, the stream beat vehemently against that house, and could not shake it, for it was founded on the rock."*

Pastor Parkey Cobern
Senior Pastor
Capstone Church
Benbrook, Texas

INTRODUCTION

We have a crack in the den wall next to the back porch of our house. I will patch the crack and repaint it, but every year it will crack again, because I have not fixed the real problem- the foundation.

The stresses and pressures in our lives can cause cracks to develop in our faith because we forget Bible teaching that we learned years ago or because we never really learned the basic scriptural principles that should form the foundation of our faith. The Bible explains this problem with our spiritual foundation:

My people are destroyed for lack of knowledge. (Hosea 4:5)

How is the foundation of my faith?

- Why is the Bible called the "Word of God"?
- Why should I trust the Bible?
- Did God create us or did we evolve, and why does it matter to me?
- Why should I pray? Does prayer make a difference?
- I don't understand when people talk about the Trinity?
- What does the Bible say about God the Father, God the Son, and God the Holy Spirit?
- The Bible says that Jesus is Savior, Lord and Christ. What is the difference between the three titles?
- How can I know God in a personal way?
- Did the nine gifts of the Holy Spirit pass away when Jesus went to heaven, or are the gifts still active today?
- Is it true that the Lord Jesus Christ will really come back at any time?
- What will happen to me and to my family and other people when Jesus does returns?

> This 10 part Bible study will help you renew your knowledge and your understanding of the foundations of your Christian faith.

Jon Dugdale
July 2013

CHAPTER ONE
THE BIBLE IS THE WORD OF THE LIVING GOD

The Bible is the Word of God, inspired by God,
without any error or fault in all its teaching.

And when He (God) had made an end of speaking with him (Moses)on Mount Sinai,
He gave Moses two tablets of the Testimony, tablets of stone,
written with the finger of God.   (Exodus 31:18)

A. God has revealed Himself to us in His Bible. [1]
 1. When you read the words of your Bible, you're reading the words out of the mouth of God.
 2. That is a tremendous reality that gives confidence to everything we do.
 3. It binds us to obedience and submission to everything the Scripture teaches.
 4. Nobody would know the truth about God, or be able to relate to God in a personal way, unless God had not first revealed Himself to us.
 5. God first commanded Moses to write God's laws and the history of God's dealings with His people in the first 5 books of the Bible.
    So it was, when Moses had completed writing the words of this law in a book,
    when they were finished, that Moses commanded the Levites, who bore the ark
    of the covenant of the Lord, saying: "Take this Book of the Law, and put it
    beside the ark of the covenant of the Lord your God ..."   (Deut. 31:24-26a)

B. The Old Testament is the revelation of God to show man: [1]
 • what God is like and Who God is
 • what God tolerates and does not tolerate (for example: pride)
 • how God desires holiness and punishes sin

C. The New Testament is the revelation of God: [1]
 • in the life of His Son
 • in the message of the coming of His Son to establish His eternal Kingdom

The Old Testament is God speaking and revealing Himself. The New Testament is God speaking and revealing His Son.

D. What the Bible is not. The Bible: [1]
- is <u>not</u> a collection of the wisdom of ancient men.
- is <u>not</u> a collection of the best of religious thinking.
- is <u>not</u> the thinking of any good or godly people or ancient people from their knowledge.

The Bible is the word of the Living God.

E. The Bible is far different than other books because its author is God. [2]

   1. The Bible declares that it is from God Himself.
      a. God used humans to write it down, but His Holy Spirit directed and helped them to write what He wanted them to say.
      b. Peter affirmed the **divine origin of biblical teaching** in 2 Peter 1.
         ... knowing this first, that no prophecy of Scripture is of any private interpretation, for prophecy never came by the will of man, but <u>holy men of God spoke as they were moved by the Holy Spirit</u>.   (2 Peter 1:20-21)

   2. Why can we believe that the Bible is God's word?
      a. Because its message is consistent from one end to the other — the message that God made us and loves us and wants us to know Him and live with Him forever.
         And if I go and prepare a place for you, I will come again and receive you to Myself; that where I am, there *you may be also.*   (John 14:3)

      b. Because when we read the Bible with an open heart and mind, we hear His voice telling us that its message is true.
      c. Most of all, because the Bible points us to Jesus Christ, the living word of God.

F. The Bible is not just one single book; it is actually a collection of 66 books. [3]
   (The word "Bible" comes from the Greek word "biblia" which means "the books or scrolls")

   1. **39** books were written **before** Christ came. **27** books were written **after** Christ came.
      a. All together, these books are the record, interpretation, and expression of God's disclosure of Himself and His relationship with His children.

    b. God included the good and the bad in His records of His dealings with His people. Including sinful people that Jesus was descended from such as: Adam & Eve, Cain who slew Abel, and Rahab who was a prostitute in Jericho who was the great, great, grandmother of King David who committed adultery and murder.

2. These 66 books were written by **40 different authors**.
    a. a farmer, a doctor, a king, shepherds, fishermen, prophets, and others

3. These 66 books were written over a period of 1,600 years.
    a. in **3 different languages**:   Hebrew, Greek, and Aramaic
    b. on **3 different continents**:   Africa, Asia, and Europe

4. These 66 books contain **no historical errors or contradictions**, and each book has:
    a. **a common storyline**- the creation, fall, and redemption of God's people
    b. **a common theme**- God's universal love for all of humanity
       The Lord has appeared of old to me, saying:
       "Yes, I have loved you with an everlasting love;
       Therefore with loving-kindness I have drawn you."   (Jeremiah 31:3)

G. The Old and New Testaments refer to themselves as the "Word of God" [4]

1. These writings are **God's own testimony and teaching** given to mankind in a form we can use. The phrase "word of God" appears 50 times in the Old and New Testaments.

2. The Lord Jesus called the Scriptures "the word of God."
    *Jesus told the Pharisees, "(you are ...) making **the word of God** of no effect through your tradition which you have handed down."*   (Mark 7:13a)

3. Jesus Christ Himself is **the living Word of God**, the ultimate expression of God. Jesus Christ is God:
    In the beginning was the Word, and the Word was with God, and the Word was God. And the Word became flesh and dwelt among us, and we beheld His glory, the glory as of the only begotten of the Father, full of grace and truth.   (John 1: 1, 14)

    That which was <u>from the beginning</u>, which <u>we have heard</u>, which <u>we have seen</u> with our eyes, which <u>we have looked upon</u>, and <u>our hands have handled</u>, concerning <u>the Word of life</u>— the life was manifested, and we have seen, and bear witness, and declare to you that eternal life which was with the Father and was manifested to us— that which we have seen and heard we declare to you, that you also may have fellowship with us; and truly our fellowship is with the Father and with His Son Jesus Christ. And these things we write to you that your joy may be full.   (1 John 1: 1-4)

H. Jesus Christ, and His apostles who taught in His name, gave us the assurance that the Scriptures are from God. [4] *("Scriptures" means "the sacred writings of the Bible")*

1. Jesus Christ, the beloved Son of God come in the flesh, studied and knew the Old Testament and treated it as **His heavenly Father's written instruction**.

2. When Satan tempted Jesus 3 times in the desert by distorting and misusing scripture, Jesus answered each time with correct scripture starting with *"It is written"*. Example:
   Now when the tempter came to Him, he (Satan) *said,*
   "If You are the Son of God, command that these stones become bread."
   But He (Jesus) *answered and said, "It is written, 'Man shall not live by bread alone, but by every word that proceeds from the mouth of God.'"*
   (Matthew 4:3-4)

3. Jesus Christ <u>fulfilled the Word of God</u> (the law and the prophets). He said:
   "Do not think that I came to destroy the Law or the Prophets.
   I did not come to destroy but to fulfill.
   For assuredly, I say to you, till heaven and earth pass away, one jot or one tittle will by no means pass from the law till all is fulfilled."   (Matt 5:17-18)

4. <u>Paul</u> described the Old Testament as entirely "God-breathed" with each word planned by His Spirit.
   a. It is **not** the product of elevated human consciousness or enlightened human intellect, but **it is** the product of God's Spirit ("breath") just as the heavens are "God-breathed".
   <u>*All Scripture*</u> *is <u>given by inspiration of God</u>, and is profitable for doctrine, for reproof, for correction, for instruction in righteousness, that the man of God may be complete, thoroughly equipped for every good work.*
   (2 Tim. 3:16-17)

5. Peter refers to Paul's letters as Scripture when, for example, Peter wrote:
   . . . our beloved brother Paul, according to the wisdom given to him, has written to you, as also <u>in all his epistles</u>, speaking in them of these things, in which are some things hard to understand, which untaught and unstable people *twist to their own destruction, as* they do *also <u>the rest of the Scriptures</u>.*
   (2 Pet. 3:15-16)

I. How do we know the words in the Bible we read today have not been changed over the centuries? [4]

1. Manuscript evidence
   a. We have over 1,400 Greek manuscripts, or parts thereof, dating from 110 A.D.

      b. We also have over 18,000 versions of the Scriptures (a version of the Bible is when it is translated into another language). There are Syriac, Latin, Egyptian, Armenian and Georgian versions dating as early as 150 A.D.

      c. We also have the Dead Sea Scrolls found in 1947 by a shepherd boy in the Qumran Caves west of the Dead Sea.
- These scrolls were written over 220 years from 150 B.C. to 70 A.D.
- They found the entire book of Isaiah, the books of Samuel and fragments of also every other book in the Old Testament.
- Before these were found, the earliest Old Testament manuscripts were dated from 900 A.D.
- The Dead Sea Scrolls reveal the accuracy of the copyist in preserving the Word of God.
- There were only spelling and grammatical differences in the Bible texts for 1,050 years (from 150 B.C. to 900 A.D.)

2. Early church lectionaries
    a. As early as about 180 A.D., the early Church used lectionary readings in the worship services of the Church.
    b. Lectionaries were books or listings that contained a collection of scripture readings appointed for Christian or Judaic worship.
    c. These reading lessons for the public worship services contained the majority of the New Testament.
    d. These lessons show the harmony between what they quoted and our Bible today.

3. The writings of early church fathers'
    a. These were men who were appointed by the apostles or followed soon after the death of the apostles. Men like:
- Ignatius (70-110 A.D.) - Bishop of Antioch, associated with John
- Polycarp (70-156 A.D.) – Bishop of Smyrna, taught by Apostles
- Clement of Rome (90 A.D.) – knew Peter who made Clement a Bishop
- and many others

J. Canonization of Scripture- Why were some books accepted and others rejected? [5]

1. The first 5 books of the Old Testament (the Torah) that God gave to Moses were immediately recognized as sacred writings given to Moses by God.
    a. The Israelites saw Moses meet God face-to-face.
    b. The book of Joshua, written by Joshua, was accepted by the people because they saw Joshua stay in the tent with God after Moses left the tent.

> *... when Moses entered the tabernacle, that the pillar of cloud descended and stood at the door of the tabernacle, and the LORD talked with Moses.*

All the people saw the pillar of cloud standing at the tabernacle door, and all the people rose and worshiped, each man in his tent door.
So the LORD spoke to Moses face to face, as a man speaks to his friend. And he would return to the camp, but his servant Joshua the son of Nun, a young man, did not depart from the tabernacle.   (Ex. 33: 9-11)

> We should imitate Joshua's faithfulness to seek and enter into the presence of the Lord Who made us for fellowship with Him

2. "Canon" refers to the following standard by which Old and New Testaments of the Bible were judged worthy of being called the Word of God (or not worthy).
    a. First, the book had to agree with the Torah.
    b. Second, it had to be recognized as having *divine authority (inspired by God)*.
    c. Next it had to have been written by a recognized man of God *(exceptions were Esther and Hebrews)*.
    d. That their divine authority was recognized over time by the people of God in the early church.
    e. That there is a direct quote from or reference to the book in another accepted book.
    f. The book cannot have historical errors.
    g. Most important is that books of the Old Testament need to have been part of accepted Hebrew Canon at the time of Jesus Christ.
    h. The so called "lost books" from the time of Christ ("gospel;" of Mary, Thomas, Enoch) were considered only to be legends and were never accepted as canon. They were full of errors and did not compare with the sacred writings and did not pass the canon tests.

K. The whole Bible is from God - the Old Testament and the New Testament.

1. The Bible is the basis of **all truth** and the essential **guide for faith and godly living**.

2. As Christians, we should thank God for **the gift of His written Word (Old and New Testaments)**, and should be conscientious in basing our faith and life entirely and exclusively on the Bible.

> *All Scripture is given by inspiration of God, and is profitable for doctrine, for reproof, for correction, for instruction in righteousness, that the man of God may be complete, thoroughly equipped for every good work.*
> (2 Tim. 3:16-17)

> *Your word is a lamp to my feet and a light to my path.*   (Psalm 119: 105)

L. How do I start reading the Bible? [6]

If you have not been diligent about reading the Bible, but want that to change, following is one plan. There are many plans available in books and on the internet. You can try this plan, or find a different one that works for you. The most important thing is to do it! Start right away and don't put it off. The Lord desires to fellowship with you in His Word.

1. First, come up with a plan— a set time and quiet spot for reading God's Word.
   Without a plan, Satan will find ways to distract us. He knows the Bible is our map for intimacy with God, and our weapon to defeat temptation. That said, here are some ways you can begin studying Scripture.

2. Don't feel obligated to read through the Bible as you would other books.
   For some people, it's more effective to read a little from the Old Testament and New Testament each day. You might want to start in Psalms, especially if you're at a point in life when you really need encouragement.

3. As for the New Testament, the gospel of Mark might be a helpful starting place.
   It's a short book, but it provides a good scope of Jesus' life and ministry. Alongside that, or perhaps afterward, consider reading through Ephesians. It's also a brief but powerful summary of the Christian life. Of course, these are simply suggestions. God might have you begin elsewhere, depending on your personal needs.

4. While reading, expect the Holy Spirit to guide you.
   Don't schedule ahead of time the number of minutes or chapters you'll cover, but let God tell you when to stop. Read until He highlights a special passage or principle; then take time to meditate on it prayerfully.
   o *"meditate"* is from a Hebrew word that means to ponder, to talk aloud with yourself, to declare, to chew over, to study, think about, wrestle with.
   o Ask Him what He's saying to you through it.
   o Pretty soon, the Holy Spirit will give understanding and direction
   o you'll sense that He's speaking to you personally.

5. Journal
   As you let the Lord lead you, write down (for example, in a spiral binder) what you feel that He is showing you in His Word.

6. Memorize Bible verses. Go over them again and again until they become a part of you. The more you do this, the easier memorization becomes.

> After you read God's Word regularly and follow the above suggestions, and you will notice:
>   - a growing love for God's Word
>
>   - and a deep peace and contentment that can be found through no other book or author.
>
>   - Only, be sure to purpose in your heart to obey whatever the Lord tells you through Scripture.
>
>   - For then and only then will the joy of reading the Bible stay with you.

M. How deeply the Lord desires fellowship with us.

Doug White, former Pastor of Restoration Church Euless, once told of an occasion when he was spending time in the presence of the Lord in the forest. The sun was just beginning to rise, and the woods were starting to come to life.
Pastor Doug said that the Lord reminded Doug of how, every time he visited his mother in the care center, no matter whether Doug had been there one hour or four hours, his mother would say, "<u>Please</u> stay a little longer."

Doug immediately recognized and accepted the tender call and yearning of the Lord wanting to continue sweet fellowship with Doug.

What is more important than us to respond to that tender urging from the Lord asking us to "stay a little longer in His presence"?

And He walks with me, and He talks with me,
And He tells me I am His own;
And the joy we share as we tarry there,
None other has ever known.

"In the Garden", by Charles A. Miles 1913

References:

[1] MacArthur, Jr., John F., *Our God-Breathed Bible*, (2 Timothy 3:16-17), *www.gty.org*

[2] Graham, Billy. *Why is the Bible different from other books?* Tribune Media Services, 2012

[3] Carlson, Ron and Jason. *Is the Bible the Inspired Word of God?* *http://www.awakengeneration.com*

[4] Carr, Pastor Steve, *Discipleship Series*, Calvary Chapel, Arroyo Grande, CA, *http://calvaryag.org*

[5] Lutzer, Erwin W. *The Doctrines that Divide*, 1998

[6] Stanley, Dr. Charles F., *Ask Dr. Stanley*, In Touch Ministries, Inc., 2012

Chapter 1, Appendix I
The New Testament Timeline [1,2]

Paper, ink, leather, thread, and glue. Today we are so accustomed to the Bible as a singular physical artifact, that we forget Scripture did not always exist in its present form. Battles with heretics, missionary journeys, and martyrdom - among other aspects of the Bible's history - make it much more colorful than we often realize.

Knowing how the Holy Spirit led Jesus' early followers to pen and pass down the church's sacred writings can invigorate our hunger for truth and our efforts to commune with the Savior. This is a graphical account of the Christian Canon's development— canon meaning "rule" or "a standard of measurement."

The table below is a fair approximation according to available research, rather than a scholarly account, and is intended only as a general introduction. [1]

Year of Event	Event
37 BC – 4 BC BC = *Before Christ*	The reign of Herod I, a Roman client king of Israel
27 BC – 14 AD	The reign of Caesar Augustus, the first emperor of the Roman Empire
AD = *Anno Domini*	Latin for "the year of our Lord"
3 BC	The birth of Jesus
26-36 AD	Pontius Pilate the Prefect of the Roman Empire's Judaea Province
27 AD	Jesus baptized by John the Baptist
28 AD	The Transfiguration of the Lord on Mount Tabor
29 AD	John the Baptist beheaded
30 AD	Jesus crucified, buried, and resurrected. The Ascension of Jesus into Heaven.
After Pentecost	
Acts 2 tells us that on the day of Pentecost, the power of the Holy Spirit came upon the disciples, just as Jesus had promised (Acts 1:8). Anointed by God, Peter preached in Jerusalem that day, and "about 3,000 souls" repented and were baptized (Acts 2:41). These new devotees of Jesus Christ didn't yet have a New Testament to guide them, so they dedicated themselves to the apostles' oral teaching (Acts 2:42). The former disciples of Jesus relied upon the Septuagint—an ancient Greek version of the Old Testament, completed c. 150 B.C. and translated for Greek-speaking Jews. As the church began to compile sacred texts of its own, it was this translation of Hebrew Scripture that the New Testament writers would later refer to and quote.	

Year of Event	Event
34 AD	The stoning of Stephen, the first deacon appointed by the apostles. The conversion of Paul. The word Christian first used at Antioch.
37 AD	Paul travels to Jerusalem to meet with Peter
44 AD	James, brother of John, beheaded. Paul's first missionary journey to Cyprus and Asia Minor (Turkey)
49 AD	Paul's second missionary journey through Asia Minor, Macedonia, Corinth, Achaia, and Ephesus The Council of Jerusalem In the beginning, members of the church were predominantly Jewish believers. They believed Jesus had fulfilled their traditions, not nullified them, and so continued observing the customs handed down from the time of Moses. But as Gentiles began receiving the gospel of Jesus Christ, new challenges arose about how to order the fledgling church's life: Should the Gentiles have to observe certain Jewish customs, such as circumcision? To discuss what should be done, all of the leaders assembled for the first documented gathering of its kind in church history. This manner of making decisions—church-wide councils—would become a powerful tool as other important decisions needed to be made. (For more about the Council of Jerusalem, read Acts 15.)
51 AD	*Second Thessalonians* Paul writes first epistle (letter to the early church) to the *Thessalonians*-probably the earliest Christian writing to be circulated among believers.
52 AD	*Galatians* Paul's third missionary journey to Asia Minor, Ephesus, Macedonia, Achaia, and Corinth
55 AD	*First Corinthians*
56 AD	*Second Corinthians*
57 AD	Epistle to the *Romans* Paul is arrested in Jerusalem and imprisoned in Caesarea
59 AD	*Philippians*- Paul probably wrote while in prison in Rome Paul's final missionary journey and voyage to Rome
60 AD	*Ephesians, Colossians, and Philemon* Paul probably wrote these while in prison in Rome.
61 AD	*James, Gospel of Mark* Most scholars agree that Mark's gospel was written before Matthew's, the latter borrowing from the former. But which version was written first remains an issue of great debate.

Year of Event	Event
62 AD	Paul freed from prison
64 AD	*First Timothy, Titus, First Peter* The Great Fire of Rome. Emperor Nero blamed the Christians, and a great persecution ensued.
65 AD	*Gospel of Matthew*
66 AD	*Second Timothy*- Paul wrote from prison The Jerusalem church scatters to locations in Decapolis and Antioch because of persecution (Acts 8)
67 AD	*Gospel of Luke* *Hebrews* - Initially believed to have been written by Paul—a tradition still held in eastern Christian churches. Today some scholars speculate that Luke, Barnabas, and Apollos are possible candidates. Peter crucified upside down by request, feeling unworthy of dying in the same posture as the Lord Paul beheaded
68 AD	*Book of Acts, Second Peter* The death of Nero- sometime between the Great Fire of Rome and the death of Nero.
70 AD	The Romans destroy Jerusalem and the Temple
72 AD	*Jude*
86 AD	*Gospel of John*
89 AD	*First John* *Third John* - though listed as the third of John's epistles in the Bible we have today, many scholars believe it was written before 2 John.
90 AD	*Second John.* John exiled to Patmos.
92 AD	*The Revelation of John*
100 AD	The death of John, the last apostle living

Death of the Apostles: Who Took Over?   (after 100 AD)
By the time all the apostles were dead, the church had devised a way of providing pastoral leadership for believers by assigning a bishop, meaning "overseer," in each city where the church existed. While we're uncertain of who all of the apostles' followers were, we know the names of several men who rose to prominence in the church after Jesus' chosen twelve departed this life. Among the most notable was Polycarp, bishop of Smyrna, whom the apostles taught; Ignatius, bishop of Antioch, who most likely associated with John; and Clement, bishop of Rome, who presumably knew Peter and was possibly made a bishop by the former disciple himself. These are but a few of many overseers appointed by the apostles as the church's missionary efforts expanded from region to region.

Year of Event	Event
117 AD	Ignatius of Antioch martyred
144 AD	**Marcion's "Canon"** Marcion, leader of a heretical movement that believed in two Gods—one of the Old Testament who was inferior to Jesus AD Christ, the New Testament's deity—proposed the first New Testament canon, including only ten epistles and parts of Luke's gospel. Marcion's canon was one of many factors that inspired the church to create an official list of sacred writings.
155 AD	Polycarp of Smyrna martyred
165 AD	Martyrdom of Justin—often referred to today as "Justin Martyr"—a former pagan philosopher who became one of the foremost apologists of the early church
166 AD	Easter formally declared a day of celebration in the west by Soter, Bishop of Rome

Disputed Books

Some books of our present New Testament were once disputed as to authenticity. This was largely due to the geographical diversity of the church — believers were spread across the known world, and it took time for certain books to gain acceptance as genuine apostolic writings. Early believers remained guarded at times out of concern about controversial teachings and spurious texts, which were composed by false teachers but attributed to the apostles. Because of this, Hebrews, James, Jude, 2 Peter, and Revelation were once held in suspicion.

Year of Event	Event
200 AD	Martyrdom of Ireneaus, author of Against Heresies—a foundational work of Christian apologetics that is still revered today
312 AD	Constantine, ruler of the Roman Empire, converts to Christianity
313 AD	Edict of Milan grants religious freedom in the Roman Empire and the restitution of property to Christians
318 AD	Beginning of the Arian controversy—named after Arius, who claimed that Jesus Christ wasn't equally God with the Father but was a created being. His heretical beliefs led many Christians astray and provoked adherents on both sides of the controversy to violence.
321 AD	Arius excommunicated
325 AD	**First Council of Nicaea** Summoned by Constantine, this council was convened primarily to resolve the Arian controversy and in so doing preserve the unity of the empire. Here, church leaders from throughout the known world gathered to formulate the "Nicene Creed"—an official statement of orthodox belief, including the doctrine of the Trinity and Jesus' being equally God with the Father, that would be used in refuting heresy. They also devised a scheme for determining the date of Pascha (Latin derived from Hebrew for "Passover"), the eastern Christian name for Easter. Constantine requests 50 bound copies of Codex Sinaiticus (Christian Bible in Greek)

Year of Event	Event
337 AD	Constantine dies
363 AD	Council of Laodicea decides the first authoritative list of biblical books in the East
367 AD	Easter letter of Athanasius, bishop of Alexandria, lists for the first time the entire list of official New Testament books
397 AD	Third Council of Carthage publishes authoritative list of biblical books in the West
405 AD	Jerome translates Christian Bible into Latin, creating the Vulgate—the official translation of the West until the Protestant Reformation

A final note [1]

Though the Christian Canon wasn't formally fixed until the fourth century, it would be a mistake to assume that the apostolic writings we know today as the New Testament were not considered authoritative before that time.

On the contrary, fixing the Canon was born out of necessity—as a means of preserving what the Holy Spirit had led the church, through the apostles' teaching, to believe about God. It was also a way to preserve orthodox belief by distinguishing authentic apostolic writings from the counterfeits that propagated falsehoods.

When the Canon was finally formed, it was only an affirmation of what the church already held to be true.

References:

[1] Stanley, Dr. Charles F., *The Birth of a New Testament- How the Christian Canon was formed,* In Touch Ministries, Inc. 2011

[2] *http://www.intouch.org*

[3] *The New Testament Timeline,* 2009 Clay McKinney , http://www.newtestamenthistorytimeline.com/

Chapter 1, Appendix II
When was the Old Testament written and who wrote it? [1]

Book	Author	Date Written
Genesis	Moses	? - 1445 B.C.
Exodus		1445 - 1405 B.C.
Leviticus		1405 B.C.
Numbers		1444 - 1405 B.C.
Deuteronomy		1405 B.C.
Joshua	Joshua	1404-1390 B.C.
Judges	Samuel	1374-1129 B.C.
Ruth		1150? B.C.
First Samuel		1043-1011 B.C.
Second Samuel	Ezra ?	1011-1004 B.C.
First Kings	Jeremiah	971-852 B.C.
Second Kings		852-587 B.C.
First Chronicles	Ezra ?	450 - 425 B.C.
Second Chronicles		450 - 425 B.C.
Ezra	Ezra	538-520 B.C.
Nehemiah	Nehemiah	445 - 425 B.C.
Esther	Mordecai ?	465 B.C.
Job	Job ?	Between 2,000 B.C. and 1,500 B.C.

Book	Author	Date Written
Psalms Written about 1061 B.C. to 444 B.C. King David created a 4,000 piece orchestra to play during worship.	David wrote Psalms 3-9, 11-32, 34-41, 51-65, 68-70, 86, 101, 103, 108-110, 122, 124, 131, 133, 138-145 Sons of Korah wrote Psalms 42, 44-49, 84-85, 87; Asaph wrote Psalms 50, 73-83; Solomon wrote Psalms 72, 127; Heman wrote Psalm 88; Ethan wrote Psalm 89; Moses wrote 90; Hezekiah wrote Psalms 120-123, 128-130, 132, 134-136;	
Proverbs	Solomon wrote 1-29 Agur wrote 30 Lemuel wrote 31	950 - 700 B.C.
Ecclesiastes	Solomon	935 B.C.
Song of Solomon		965 B.C.
Isaiah	Isaiah	740 - 680 B.C.
Jeremiah	Jeremiah	627 - 585 B.C.
Lamentations		586 B.C.
Ezekiel	Ezekiel	593-560 B.C.
Daniel	Daniel	605-536 B.C.
Hosea	Hosea	710 B.C.
Joel	Joel	835 B.C.
Amos	Amos	755 B.C.
Obadiah	Obadiah	840 or 586 B.C.
Jonah	Jonah	760 B.C.
Micah	Micah	700 B.C.

Book	Author	Date Written
Nahum	*Nahum*	663 - 612 B.C.
Habakkuk	*Habakkuk*	607 B.C.
Zephaniah	*Zephaniah*	625 B.C.
Haggai	*Haggai*	520 B.C.
Zechariah	*Zechariah*	520 - 518 B.C.
Malachi	*Malachi*	450 - 600 B.C.

References:

[1] Slick, Matt, *Christian Apologetics and Research Ministry*, 1995,
http://carm.org/when-was-bible-written-and-who-wrote-it

CHAPTER TWO
GOD IS THE CREATOR AND SUSTAINER OF EVERYTHING

You are worthy, O Lord,
To receive glory and honor and power;
For YOU CREATED ALL THINGS,
And BY YOUR WILL THEY EXIST AND WERE CREATED.
(Revelation 4:11)

A. <u>God created everything</u> **by His Word … by His command … from nothing before anything existed.**

> In **the beginning God created** the heavens and the earth.
> The earth was **without form**, and void;
>   and **darkness** was on the face of the deep.
> And **the Spirit of God** was hovering (sweeping, moving)
>   over the face of the waters.
> Then **God said**, *"Let there be light"; and* **there was** *light.*   (Genesis 1: 1-3)

1. The act of creation is a great mystery to us. There is more in it than we can understand.

2. To say that God created "everything out of nothing" is to confess the mystery, not to explain it.

3. Believing what the Bible says about God creating everything requires us to <u>receive it by faith in God</u> and <u>faith in His Word</u>.

> *<u>By faith</u> we understand that the worlds were framed by the word of God, so that the things which are seen were not made of things which are visible.*
> (Hebrews 11:3)

B. All things were created <u>through</u> Christ Jesus and <u>for</u> Christ Jesus.

> In the beginning was the Word,
>   and the Word was with God,
>   and <u>the Word was God</u>.
> He was in the beginning with God.
> <u>All things were made through Him,</u>
>   <u>and without Him nothing was made that was made</u>.   (John 1:1-3)

1. The verses above from John declare that Jesus is <u>the One who made all of creation</u>.

2. Everything was created by Him and for Him and for His pleasure:
   *He (Jesus) is the **image** of the invisible God, the firstborn over all creation.*
   For <u>by Him all things were created</u> that are in heaven and that are on earth,
   visible and invisible, whether thrones or dominions or principalities or powers.
   <u>All things were created through Him and for Him</u>.   (Colossians 1: 15-16)

   ... and <u>for thy pleasure</u> they are and were created.   (Revelation 4:11b, *KJV*)
       (God takes pleasure in us)

3. In the Colossians verse above, the Greek word for **image** means Jesus is an
   <u>exact revelation and representation</u> of God the Father.
   "If you had known Me, you would have known My Father also;
   *   and from now on you know Him and have seen Him."*
   Philip said to Him, "Lord, show us the Father, and it is sufficient for us."
   *   Jesus said to him,*
   "Have I been with you so long, and yet you have not known Me, Philip?
   <u>He who has seen Me has seen the Father</u>... "   (John 14: 7-9a)
       (This means we can walk with Jesus for years and <u>not really know Him</u>)

4. No fellowship with robots- Human beings were created by God and are not
   robots, but were made with <u>free will</u> capable of free decisions for which they are
   morally accountable to their Maker.

5. The fallen angel Satan and the other angels, who rebelled against God, were all
   created with <u>free will</u> by God. God, the Creator of all, is greater than all of them.
   (1 Tim 3:6; double reference in Isaiah 14:12-14 and Ezekiel 28:12-18 referring
   to ancient kings and to the fall of Satan)

C. We are God's special creation from all He has made [1]

   Then God said, "Let Us make man in Our image, according to Our likeness;
                                                                (Gen 1:26a)
       (We are God's special creation)

1. Here is the tender account of how man took his first breath, aided entirely by
   the Creator, who shared His own breath with him.
   *And **the LORD God formed man** of the dust of the ground,*
   *and **breathed into his nostrils the breath of life**;*
   *and **man became a living being**.*   (Gen 2:7)

       ("Breathe" means "inner soul or spirit")

2. The original Hebrew word for **formed** means- to mould into a form, especially like a potter does.

   " Your hands have made me and fashioned me..."   (Job 10:8a)

   *"For You **formed** my inward parts;*
   You covered me in my mother's womb.   I will praise You,
   for I am fearfully and wonderfully made   (Psalm 139:13-14)

   But now, O Lord, You are our Father;
   We are the clay, and You our potter;
   And all we are the work of Your hand.   (Isaiah 64:8)

3. Intimate creation
   a. God formed us with His hands from the dust of the earth.
   b. We lay lifeless until the Lord God breathed His breath into our nostrils

4. At creation, God gave us the precious gift of life that only God has to give.
   a. So God created man in His image with self-consciousness, personality, rationality, intelligence, creativity, relationships
   b. God also created the "spiritual" nature of man (self-image, moral consciousness, abstract reasoning, language, will, religious nature, etc.). We are supernatural creations totally distinct from mere biological lives created by God.
   c. God gave him sovereignty over the entire created world and all its vast resources, so that man could bring up out of this rich, rich planet immense demonstrations of God's imparted marvelous abilities to man rationally and creatively and relationally.

5. The Potter and the Clay
   Do we doubt our reason for being here?   Why God made us?

   Shall the potter be esteemed as the clay;
   For shall the thing made say of him who made it, "He did not make me"?
   Or shall the thing formed say of him who formed it, "He has no understanding"?   (Isaiah 29:16)

   But indeed, O man, who are you to reply against God?
   Will the thing formed say to him who formed it,
   "Why have you made me like this?"   (Romans 9:20)

D. Let us praise God as the Creator for the marvelous order, variety, and beauty of His works.

1. The heavens and the earth, the air we breathe, mankind and all life did not happen by accident. We did not evolve from accident by an unguided act of nature. Did the "evolution god" cause chance to make fruits and veggies attractive and tasty for us? No; God created the amazing variety of flowers and colors and trees. Delicious fruits such as apples, grapes, peaches, watermelon, honey, molasses, walnuts and the beauty of the earth are not by chance. Materials that we use did not happen by chance- wood, iron, gold, glass. The miracle of our marvelous eye did not just happen.

2. Trust We can trust God as the Supreme Lord over all - Who has <u>an eternal plan</u> covering all events and destinies without exception – Who has the desire and the power to redeem us, re-create us and renew us.

God thinks about me

    For I know the thoughts that I think toward you, says the LORD,
    thoughts of peace and not of evil, to give you a future and a hope.
    Then you will call upon Me and go and pray to Me, and I will listen to you.
    And you will seek Me and find Me,
    when you search for Me with all your heart. (Jeremiah 29:11-12)

3. Let this trust become real as we remember that it is <u>God the Almighty Creator</u> that we are trusting.

    *Let them **praise the name of the LORD**,*
    For He commanded and they were created. (Psalm 148:5)
    He gives to all life, breath, and all things…
    for in Him we live and move and have our being (Acts 17:25, 28)

E. God as Creator or evolution as our god?

1. There is <u>not any mention</u> of evolution anywhere in the Bible.
    a. <u>no mention</u> of God watching man evolve from other life forms.
    b. <u>no mention</u> of pre-human, apelike ancestors.

2. Evolution- World Book Encyclopedia definition:
    "The idea that living things evolved from non-living matter and changed through the ages is called the theory of evolution. According to this theory, the first single-celled organisms appeared about 3 or 4 billion years ago. As time passed, more complex organisms gradually developed specialized characteristics that helped them adapt to their environment. The evolutionary process eventually produced all the species that inhabit the earth."

3. The Astronaut and the Pocket Watch - a story I made up to jokingly illustrate how inconceivably difficult it is to believe the theory of evolution.

>   *The first man we send to the moon is walking on the moon and finds a pocket watch. Completely amazed, he returns to earth with the watch and hands it to the smartest scientists the world has. Starting with the science of evolution that they have believed their entire life, the scientists perform a detailed study and analysis of the pocket watch found on the moon.*
>   *After lengthy study and meeting, the scientists release a statement with the results of their research that states that all of the scientists agree that the moon watch evolved over billions of years. First, the gold and silver and brass materials oozed out of the moon's surface and evolved into gears and bearings. Likewise, the other parts such as the case and the chain evolved through many shapes until they are what you see now. Amazingly, the glass also evolved over time to form the crystal. Other materials came together to form the watch's white face and the 12 intricate black numbers equally spaced on the watch's face. Most amazing to the entire group of scientists was that a storm of energy on the moon's surface caused the watch to start running and ticking on its own and to keep perfect time even unto the current day.*

Yes, the story is ridiculous! But the watch story is **much easier to believe** than the idea that the marvelous creation that we are **"somehow just happened on its own."**
Are we more complex than a watch? Of course we are!

4. Evolution has become a god to scientists and to society. A majority of people believe that this "god" called "evolution" directed life to accidentally come from nothing and evolve into creatures that, in turn, evolved eyes and other senses as needed, organs and lungs and hearts as needed, and brains to cause the lungs and hearts to function until our lifetimes end. This acceptance of the god of evolution requires greater faith than to accept the real truth- that God created everything as declared in His Word.

F. Creation and the theory of Evolution- The Science of Each

1. The following chapter 2 appendices outline a short overview of evolution science.

2. These are informative from the standpoint of science, but we must always look back to what the Bible says about creation, and we must always come back to our faith in God- not be concerned or confused by what scientists interpret about what they see.

> *For since the creation of the world, His invisible attributes are clearly seen,*
>   *being understood by the things that are made,*
>   *even His eternal power and Godhead,*
>   *so that they are without excuse.*   (Romans 1:20)

References:

[1]   MacArthur, Jr., John F., *The Creation of Man (Genesis 2:4-7)*, 1999
      http://www.jcsm.org/StudyCenter/john_macarthur/90-226.htm

Chapter 2, Appendix I
Evidence to Reject Evolution

God's position on evolution is in the first chapter of the Bible

A. The evidence is that <u>like kinds</u> always give rise to <u>like kinds</u> of living things.

1. In all the years of observing nature, scientists have never seen this law broken or violated. The Bible clearly supports this evidence.

    So God created great sea creatures and every living thing that moves, with which the waters abounded, <u>according to their kind</u>, and every winged bird <u>according to its kind</u>. And God saw that it was good. Then God said, "Let the earth bring forth the living creature <u>according to its kind</u>: cattle and creeping thing and beast of the earth, <u>each according to its kind</u>"; and it was so.
    (Gen. 1:21,24)

2. Dr. Henry Morris III (co-founder of the Institute of Creation Research- see chapter 2 appendix II) states, "What we see is an array of distinct "kinds" of plants and animals with many varieties within each kind, but with very clear and distinct gaps between the kinds."

3. Evolution is not variation within a species, but is movement from one species to an entirely new one. The variation that Darwin observed on the Galapagos Islands resulted from isolated animal life that had only developed variations within the species or kind. But, these animals had not become a new species. (birds had not become reptiles).

4. Dr. Morris declares, "All present living kinds of plants and animals have remained fixed since creation, except for extinctions, and genetic variation in originally created kinds has only occurred within narrow limits."

B. The theory of evolution has no evidence of transitional forms in the fossil record.

1. A transitional form means that you should see in the fossil record the conversion of one species transitioning into a new species.
    a. For example: a fish into an amphibian, an amphibian to a reptile, reptiles to birds, or an ape into a man
    b. This of course would be powerful and essential evidence to prove evolution.

2. Even Charles Darwin wrote in chapter 6 ("Difficulties with the Theory") of his "Origin of the Species" that these transitional forms <u>had to be found to prove his ideas</u>.

3. The fact is that there have been <u>no transitional forms found to date</u> from the literally billions and billions of fossils already unearthed.

4. Instead, the fossils do reveal that all highly complex forms of life <u>abruptly show up in the fossil record</u> without evolutionary ancestors (transitional forms).
    a. To get around the lack of transitional forms in the fossil record, modern anthropologists came up with a new hypothesis that teaches that the species did not gradually evolve, but evolved from one species to another in giant steps, so there would be no transitional forms in the fossil record.
    b. <u>There is no evidence to support this idea either.</u>
    c. They have they <u>not found</u> transitional forms in the fossil record <u>because there are none.</u>

C. Today, classrooms <u>only</u> teach Evolution

1. Illustrations from current anthropologists cover the walls of every science classroom in America (from elementary all the way through university) depicting the transition of apes to men.

2. Evolution is taught as fact instead of as a theory in almost all schools, and teachers and scientists who challenge evolution are branded as ignorant, sometimes losing their jobs and their professional futures.

D. Is Neanderthal In Our Family Tree?   *by John D. Morris, Ph.D.*
ONE TRANSITION THEORY BUSTED

1. The first Neanderthal bones were unearthed in 1856 and were soon touted as supporting Darwin's 1859 theory of human descent from the animals.

2. Since then, Neanderthals have been presented as beetle-browed, bowlegged, brutes-half ape and half man. School students and museum visitors worldwide still believe that this "caveman" was a sub-human ancestor.

3. It surprises many to find out that in recent years, Neanderthal has been upgraded to <u>fully human—an ethnic group</u> (such as Native American, African, Eskimo (Inuit), Dutch) with certain distinctive characteristics, but a bonafide member of *Homo sapiens.*   (discovered through analysis of DNA)

4. The only controversy, which remains, is whether or not the Neanderthal group went extinct or merged with other humans.

5. The *Homo sapiens* designation was given after it was recognized that Neanderthals had, on average, a larger brain size than modern man, with a fully developed language center.

6. Culturally, he cared for his sick and elderly, buried his dead, employed art and religious rites, appreciated agriculture, clothing, and music.

7. His cultural level was "primitive" compared to twentieth century technology, but not all that different from many people groups worldwide in recent centuries.

E. Evolution <u>cannot explain</u> the "organs of extreme perfection and complication."

1. Darwin admitted in Chapter 6 of "Origin of the Species" that it was hard to accept the fact that natural selection could produce the organs in our bodies that we marvel at.
2. Darwin declared, "To suppose that the eye, with all its inimitable contrivances for adjusting the focus to different distances, for admitting different amounts of light, and for the correction of spherical and chromatic aberration, could have been formed by natural selection, seems, <u>I freely confess, absurd in the highest degree possible</u>."

3. In other words, if the eye had thousands of mutations over thousands of generations to naturally select out the humans that couldn't see well, how could a human survive at all if he or she couldn't see very well?

4. Darwin's own doubts also bring us to the same conclusion of the psalmist:
   For You formed my inward parts;
   You covered me in my mother's womb.
   I will praise You, for I am fearfully and wonderfully made;
   marvelous are Your works, and that my soul knows very well.

   (Ps. 139:13-14)

References:

[1] Carr, Pastor Steve, *Apologetics Series*, Calvary Chapel, Arroyo Grande, CA,
   http://calvaryag.org/index.php?option=com_content&task=view&id=75&Itemid=46

Chapter 2, Appendix II
Institute for Creation Research (ICR) – Dallas, Texas

- ICR conducts laboratory, field, theoretical, and library research on projects that seek to understand the science of origins and earth history.
- With 30 years experience in graduate education, first through the California-based science education program (1981-2011), and now through the M.C.Ed. degree program at the School of Biblical Apologetics, ICR trains men and women to do real-world apologetics with a foundation of biblical authority and creation science.
- ICR speaks to over 200 groups each year through seminars and conferences.
- Many of the faculty are contributing authors to ICR's new Science Education Essentials curriculum products for Christian K-12 teachers.
- ICR produces and/or publishes books, films, periodicals, and other media, including:
  - *Acts & Facts*, a full-color monthly magazine with a readership of over 200,000, providing articles relevant to science, apologetics, education, and worldview issues.
  - daily devotional *Days of Praise* with over 300,000 readers worldwide.
  - Three radio programs produced by ICR on some 1,500 outlets around the world.

ICR Principles of Biblical Creationism

Here are two of the ICR principles of Biblical Creation:
- The Creator of the universe is a triune God: Father, Son, and Holy Spirit. There is only one eternal and transcendent God, the source of all being and meaning, and He exists in three Persons, each of whom participated in the work of creation.
- The Bible, consisting of the 39 canonical books of the Old Testament and the 27 canonical books of the New Testament, is the divinely-inspired revelation of the Creator to man. Its unique, plenary, verbal inspiration guarantees that these writings, as originally and miraculously given, are infallible and completely authoritative on all matters with which they deal, free from error of any sort, scientific and historical as well as moral and theological.

ICR Principles of Scientific Creationism

Here are two of the ICR principles of Scientific Creationism:
- The physical universe of space, time, matter, and energy has not always existed, but was supernaturally created by a transcendent personal Creator who alone has existed from eternity.
- The first human beings did not evolve from an animal ancestry, but were specially created in fully human form from the start. Furthermore, the "spiritual" nature of man (self-image, moral consciousness, abstract reasoning, language, will, religious nature, etc.) is itself a supernaturally created entity distinct from mere biological life.

References:

[1] Institute for Creation Research (ICR) and the School of Biblical Apologetics, 1806 Royal Lane. Dallas, Texas 75229, *http://www.icr.org*

Chapter 2, Appendix III
The Creation Evidence Museum- Glen Rose, Texas

The Creation Evidence Museum is a non-profit educational museum chartered in Texas in 1984 for the purpose of researching and displaying scientific evidence for creation. As such, the museum sponsors paleontological and archaeological excavations in addition to other extensive research projects.

Carl Baugh, the museum's Founder and Director, originally came to Glen Rose, Texas to critically examine claims of human and dinosaur co-habitation.

- He conducted extensive excavations along the Paluxy River, with appropriate permission of the landowners. These original excavations yielded human footprints among dinosaur footprints (see the Director's doctoral dissertation).
- He helped establish a museum to appropriately display this evidence, along with sustained excavations and other areas of scientific research for creation.

Scientific Evidence for Creation

A tremendous amount of evidence for design and recent creation is available for detailed study.

- Romans 1:20 states: *"For the invisible things of him from the creation are clearly seen, being understood by the things that are made, even his eternal power and Godhead: so that they are without excuse."*
- Scientific evidence for creation abounds in areas of objective observation.
- Scholars in various scientific disciplines have written about the incredible complexity in living systems and the structure of the universe.
- This complexity is beyond the possibility of natural development.

References:

[1] Creation Evidence Museum, P.O. Box 309, Glen Rose, Texas 76043,
   http://184.154.224.5/~creatio1/index.php?option=com_content&task=view&id=1&Itemid=3

CHAPTER THREE
THE FATHER, THE SON AND THE HOLY SPIRIT

God is three distinct and eternal individuals making up one God -
the Father, the Son and the Holy Spirit, spoken of as the Trinity.

And Jesus came and spoke to them, saying, "All authority has been given to Me
in heaven and on earth. Go therefore and make disciples of all the nations,
*baptizing them in **the name of the Father and of the Son and of the Holy Spirit***
teaching them to observe all things that I have commanded you;
and lo, I am with you always, even to the end of the age. Amen.
Matthew 28:18-20

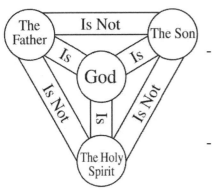

Our Triune God [1]

- Although the fullness of the Trinity is far beyond human comprehension, it is how God has revealed Himself in Scripture—as one God eternally existing in three Persons.

- The Divine essence of God subsists wholly and indivisibly, simultaneously and eternally, in the three members of the one Godhead—the Father, Son, and Holy Spirit.

A. The Scriptures are clear that the Father, Son, and Holy Spirit together are one and only one God

1. Jesus declared that the Father and the Son are one.

   "I and My Father are one."

   The Jews answered Him, saying, "For a good work we do not stone You, but for blasphemy, and because You, being a Man, make Yourself God."

   (John 10:30,33)

2. The Father and the Spirit are one.

   Do you not know that you are the temple of God and that the Spirit of God dwells in you? (1 Corinthians 3:16)

3. The Son and the Spirit are one.

   But you are not in the flesh but in the Spirit, if indeed the Spirit of God dwells in you. Now if anyone does not have the Spirit of Christ, he is not His.

   (Romans 8:9)

4. The Father, Son, and Spirit are one.

   Before Jesus was arrested and crucified, He told the Disciples:

   *"And I will pray **the Father**, and He will give you another Helper, that He may abide with you forever—**the Spirit of truth**, whom the world cannot receive, because it neither sees Him nor knows Him; but **you know Him, for He dwells with you and will be in you**. I will not leave you orphans; I will come to you."*

   *Jesus answered and said to him, "If anyone loves Me, he will keep My word; and My Father will love him, and **We** (the Father, Jesus the Son, and the Holy Spirit) **will come to him and make Our home with him."***

   (John 14:16-18, 23)

B. The Bible shows that God is a Trinity of Persons.

1. In the Old Testament, the Bible implies the idea of the Trinity in several ways.
   a. The Hebrew title Elohim ("God"), for instance, is a plural noun which can suggest multiplicity (Gen. 1:26).
   b. This corresponds to the fact that the plural pronoun ("us") is sometimes used of God.

      *Let **us** make man in our image*   (Gen 1:26)
      *Let **us** go down …*   (Gen. 11:7)
      *Also, I heard the voice of the Lord say, "Who will go for **us**?"* (Isaiah 6:8)

   c. There are places in which God's name is applied to more than one Person in the same text.

      The Lord said to my Lord,
      "Sit at My right hand,
      Till I make Your enemies Your footstool."   (Ps. 110:1)

      Then the Lord rained brimstone and fire on Sodom and Gomorrah, from the Lord out of the heavens.   (Gen. 19:24)

2. The term the "Trinity" is a basic doctrine of orthodox Christianity, yet the word "Trinity" itself is not found anywhere in the Bible.
   a. The doctrine of the Trinity is arrived at by looking at the whole of scripture – not just in a single verse.
   b. God is infinite, eternal, and unchangeable, and is revealed to us as the Father, Son, and Holy Spirit.

3. And there are also passages where all three divine Persons are seen at work.

> *"Come near to Me, hear this:*
> *I have not spoken in secret from the beginning;*
> *From the time that it was, I was there.*
> *And now the Lord GOD and His Spirit have sent Me*   (Isaiah 48:16)

Isaiah was speaking of the Messiah, who would come in the future.

> *"The Spirit of the Lord God* is *upon Me,*
> *Because the Lord has anointed Me*
> *To preach good tidings to the poor;*
> *He has sent Me to heal the brokenhearted,*
> *To proclaim liberty to the captives,*
> *And the opening of the prison to* those who are *bound;*   (Isaiah 61:1)

4. The New Testament builds significantly on these truths, revealing them more explicitly.

   a. The Lord Jesus in Matthew 28 designates all three Persons of the Trinity:

   > *"Go therefore and make disciples of all the nations, baptizing them in the name of <u>the Father</u> and <u>the Son</u> and <u>the Holy Spirit</u>."*
   > (Matthew 28:19)

   b. In his apostolic benediction to the Corinthians, Paul underscored this same reality. He wrote:

   > *The grace of <u>the Lord Jesus Christ</u>, and <u>the love of God</u> [the Father], and the fellowship of <u>the Holy Spirit</u>, be with you all.*   (2 Cor. 13:14)

C. Other New Testament passages also spell out the glorious truth of the Triune God

> *... that I might be a <u>minister of Jesus Christ</u> to the Gentiles, ministering <u>the gospel of God</u>, that the offering of the Gentiles might be acceptable, <u>sanctified by the Holy Spirit</u>.*
>
> *Now I beg you, brethren, through <u>the Lord Jesus Christ</u>, and through <u>the love of the Spirit</u>, that you strive together with me in <u>prayers to God</u> for me*
> (Romans 15:16, 30)
>
> *Now He who establishes us with you <u>in Christ</u> and has <u>anointed us is God</u>, who also has sealed us and given us <u>the Spirit</u> in our hearts as a guarantee.*
> (2 Cor. 1:21–22)
>
> *For <u>through Him</u>* (through Jesus) *we both have access by <u>one Spirit</u> to <u>the Father</u>.*
> (Eph. 2:18)

D. In describing the Trinity, the New Testament clearly distinguishes three Persons who are all simultaneously active.

1. At Christ's baptism, all three Persons were active at the same time, with the Son being baptized, the Spirit descending, and the Father speaking from Heaven.

   *When He had been baptized, **Jesus** came up immediately from the water;*
   and behold, the heavens were opened to Him,
   *and He saw **the Spirit of God** descending like a dove and alighting upon Him.*
   *And suddenly **a voice came from heaven**, saying,*
   *"This is **My beloved Son**, in whom I am well pleased."*   (Matt 3:16-17)

2. Jesus Himself prayed to the Father   (Matt. 6:9 The Lord's Prayer))
   a. taught that His will was distinct from His Father's will:
      "... not as I will, but as You will"   (Matt. 26:39)
   b. promised that He would ask the Father to send the Holy Spirit   (John 14:16)
   c. and asked the Father to glorify Him   (John 17:5)
   d. These actions would not make sense unless the Father and the Son were two distinct Persons.

3. God the Son and God the Holy Spirit
   a. **Jesus, who is our Advocate, intercedes before the Father on behalf of believers**

      My little children, these things I write to you, so that you may not sin.
      And if anyone sins, we have an Advocate with the Father,
      Jesus Christ the righteous.   (1 John 2:1)

   b. **The Holy Spirit also intercedes for us before the Father on behalf of believers**

      Likewise the Spirit also helps in our weaknesses.
      For we do not know what we should pray for as we ought,
      but the Spirit Himself makes intercession for us with groanings
      which cannot be uttered.   (Rom. 8:26)
   c. Again, the distinctness of each Person is in view.

E. God the Father

1. God as Father reigns over all of His universe with providential care.
   "providential" means divine guidance or care: the power guiding us; the power sustaining us

2. He is all-powerful, all-loving, all-knowing, and all-wise.

3. He is fatherly in attitude toward all men, but is Father, indeed, to those who have become children of God through Jesus Christ, Who will deliver them into the Father's hands.

4. Jesus often spoke of God as His Father, and the apostles frequently spoke of "God the Father".

Grace to you and peace from God our Father and the Lord Jesus Christ.
(1 Cor.1:3)

(Jesus said) "In this manner, therefore, pray:
Our Father in heaven, Hallowed be Your name." (Matthew 6:9)

And He (Jesus) said to them, "It is not for you to know times or seasons which the Father has put in His own authority. (Acts 1:7)

For as many as are led by the Spirit of God, these are sons of God. For you did not receive the spirit of bondage again to fear, but you received the Spirit of adoption by whom we cry out, "Abba, Father." (Romans 8:14-15)

... yet for us there is one God, the Father, of whom are all things, and we for Him; and one Lord Jesus Christ, through whom are all things, and through whom we live. (1 Corinthians 8:6)

Then comes the end, when He delivers the kingdom to God the Father, when He puts an end to all rule and all authority and power. (1 Corinthians 15: 24)

... one God and Father of all, who is above all, and through all, and in you all.
(Ephesians 4:6)

F. God the Son
(also see chapter 4 of this Study Guide for more about Jesus Christ- God the Son)

1. The Lord Jesus Christ, the eternal Son of God, became man without ceasing to be God, having been conceived of the Holy Spirit and born of a virgin, in order that He might <u>reveal God</u> and <u>redeem sinful man</u>.

2. He redeemed us by voluntarily giving Himself as a sinless, substitutionary sacrifice on the cross, thereby satisfying God's righteous judgment against sin.

Paul wrote in 1 Cor. 15: 3-6a:

*For I delivered to you first of all that which I also received: that **Christ died for our sins** according to the Scriptures, and that He was buried, and that He **rose again the third day** according to the Scriptures, and that He was seen by Cephas, then by the twelve. After that He was **seen by over five hundred brethren at once"***

3. After His bodily resurrection from the grave, He ascended to the right hand of His Father, where He intercedes on behalf of those who trust Him.

4. Thomas acknowledged Jesus as, *"My Lord and my God"* (John 20:28)

5. Both Peter and Paul spoke of Jesus as *"our God and Savior"*

Simon Peter, a bondservant and apostle of Jesus Christ,
To those who have obtained like precious faith with us by the righteousness of
our God and Savior Jesus Christ   (2 Pet. 1:1)

For the grace of God that brings salvation has appeared to all men, teaching
us that, of our great God and Savior Jesus Christ   (Titus 2:11-13)

6. Yet the New Testament also makes the distinction between the Father and the Son as two very different persons.

7. The Bible shows us that they love one another, speak to each other, and seek to glorify each other.   Jesus prayed to the Father:

"I do not pray for these alone,
but also for those who will believe in Me through their word;
that they all may be one, as You, Father, are in Me, and I in You;
that they also may be one in Us, that the world may believe that You sent Me."
                                                (John 17:20-21)

And the angel answered (Mary) *and said to her, "**The Holy Spirit** will come*
*upon you, and the power of **the Highest** will overshadow you; therefore, also,*
*that Holy One who is to be born will be called **the Son of God**.*
                                                (Luke 1:34-35)

*In the beginning was the Word, and the Word was with God, and **the Word***
***was God. He was in the beginning with God**. And the Word became flesh and*
dwelt among us, and we beheld His glory, the glory as of the only begotten of
*the Father, full of grace and truth. No one has seen God at any time. The **only***
***begotten Son**, who is in the bosom of **the Father**, He has declared Him.*
                                                (John 1:1, 2, 14, 18)

*... being justified freely by His grace through the redemption that is in **Christ***
***Jesus, whom God set forth** as a propitiation by His blood, through faith, to*
demonstrate His righteousness, because in His forbearance God had passed
over the sins that were previously committed, to demonstrate at the present
time His righteousness, that He might be just and the justifier of the one who
has faith in Jesus.   (Romans 3:24-26)

... or what the law could not do in that it was weak through the flesh, **God** *did by sending* **His own Son** *in the likeness of sinful flesh, on account of sin: He condemned sin in the flesh,*   (Romans 8:3)

G. God the Holy Spirit

1. The Bible refers to the Holy Spirit as God:

    But Peter said, "Ananias, why has Satan filled your heart **to lie to the Holy Spirit** *and keep back part of the price of the land for yourself?*
    While it remained, was it not your own?
    And after it was sold, was it not in your own control?
    Why have you conceived this thing in your heart?
    You have **not lied to men but to God.***"*   (Acts 5:3-4)

2. The Holy Spirit is the Divine Person who convicts the world of sin (righteousness and judgment).

3. He alone brings new life to those who are spiritually dead.

4. He baptizes (or places) all believers into the one true Church, which is the Body of Christ.

5. He indwells them permanently, seals them unto the day of final redemption, bestows spiritual gifts upon them, and fills (controls) those who are yielding to Him.

6. Every believer is called to live in the power of the indwelling Holy Spirit so that he will not fulfill the lust of the flesh but will bear fruit to the glory of God.

    Jesus answered, "Most assuredly, I say to you, unless one is born of water and the Spirit, he cannot enter the kingdom of God. That which is born of the flesh is flesh, and that which is born of the Spirit is spirit. Do not marvel that I said to you, 'You must be born again.' The wind blows where it wishes, and you hear the sound of it, but cannot tell where it comes from and where it goes. So is everyone who is born of the Spirit."
                                                                          (John 3:5-8)

    And I will pray the Father, and He will give you another Helper, that He may abide with you forever— the Spirit of truth, whom the world cannot receive, because it neither sees Him nor knows Him; but you know Him, for He dwells with you and will be in you.   (John 14:16-17)

(Also, see chapter 5 of this Study Guide for more about God the Holy Spirit.)

H. What does it mean for you and me to have a correct understand of God's nature?

1. Knowing Who God is will draw us to a spiritual and personal relationship with Him.

2. We will never be deceived by cultic teachings of who God is.
    a. James warned us not to be deceived. This means we <u>can</u> be deceived.
    b. We are called to come to the knowledge of God.
        ... we should no longer be children, tossed to and fro and carried about with every wind of doctrine, by the trickery of men, in the cunning craftiness of deceitful plotting.   (Ephesians 4:14)

3. The Bible is clear that there is only one God Who always has existed as a Trinity of Persons—the Father, the Son, and the Spirit.

4. To deny or misunderstand the Trinity is to deny or misunderstand the very nature of God Himself.

> *May the grace of **the Lord Jesus Christ**, and **the love of God**, and the fellowship of **the Holy Spirit** be with you all.*   (2 Cor. 13:14)

Praise God, from Whom all blessings flow;
Praise Him, all creatures here below;
Praise Him above, ye heavenly host;
Praise Father, Son, and Holy Ghost.

"The Doxology", by Thomas Ken 1674

References:

[1] MacArthur, Jr., John F., *Our Triune God, 1-3 John*: The MacArthur New Testament Commentary, Moody Publishers, 2007

[2] Carr, Pastor Steve. *Discipleship*, Calvary Chapel, Arroyo Grande, CA., *www.calvaryag.org*

Chapter 3, Appendix I
Scriptures about the Triune God

How the doctrine of the Trinity is supported in Scripture,
and how each Person of the Trinity has the attributes of God.

The Triune God (The Trinity)			
Each Person	**Father**	**Son**	**Holy Spirit**
is called God	*Grace to you and peace from **God our Father** and the Lord Jesus Christ.* (Phil. 1:2)	*In the beginning was the Word, and the Word was with God, and **the Word was God.*** (John 1:1) *And the Word became flesh and dwelt among us, and we beheld His glory, the glory as of the only begotten of the Father, full of grace and truth.* (John 1:14) *For in Him dwells all the fullness of the Godhead bodily.* (Col. 2:9)	*But Peter said, "Ananias, why has Satan filled your heart to lie **to the Holy Spirit** and keep back part of the price of the land for yourself? …* *You have not lied to men but to God."* (Acts 5:3-4)
is Creator	*In the beginning **God created the heavens and the earth.*** (Gen. 1:1)	*He was in the world, and **the world was made through Him**, and the world did not know Him.* (John 1:10)	***The Spirit of God has made me**, and the breath of the Almighty gives me life.* (Job 33:4)
	Isaiah 64:8; Heb. 3:4	Col. 1:15-17; John 1:1-3	Job 26:13; Psalm 104:30
sanctifies the believer	*Jude, a bondservant of Jesus Christ, and brother of James, to those who are called, **sanctified by God the Father**, and preserved in Jesus Christ …* (Jude 1:1) 1 Thess. 5:23	*To the church of God which is at Corinth, to those **who are sanctified in Christ Jesus**, called to be saints, with all who in every place call on the name of Jesus Christ our Lord, both theirs and ours* (1 Cor. 1:2) Heb. 2:11	*Peter, an apostle of Jesus Christ, to the pilgrims of the Dispersion … according to the foreknowledge of God the Father, in **sanctification of the Spirit**, for obedience and sprinkling of the blood of Jesus Christ* (1 Peter 1:2)

The Triune God (The Trinity)			
Each Person	**Father**	**Son**	**Holy Spirit**
is Love	For God so loved the world that He gave His only begotten Son, that whoever believes in Him should not perish but have everlasting life. (John 3:16)	Husbands, love your wives, just as Christ also loved the church and gave Himself for her (Eph. 5:25)	Now I beg you, brethren, through the Lord Jesus Christ, and through the love of the Spirit, that you strive together with me in prayers to God for me, (Rom. 15:30)
is everywhere	" Am I a God near at hand," says the LORD, and not a God afar off? Can anyone hide himself in secret places, so I shall not see him?" says the Lord; "Do I not fill heaven and earth?" says the Lord. (Jer. 23:23-24) "But will God indeed dwell on the earth? Behold, heaven and the heaven of heavens cannot contain You. How much less this temple which I have built!" (1 Kings 8:27)	For where two or three are gathered together in My name, I am there in the midst of them. (Matt. 18:20)	Where can I go from Your Spirit? Or where can I flee from Your presence? (Psalm 139:7-10)
is all knowing	For if our heart condemns us, God is greater than our heart, and knows all things. (1 John 3:20)	Now we are sure that You know all things, and have no need that anyone should question You. By this we believe that You came forth from God." And Peter said to Jesus,"Lord, You know all things…" (John 16:30; 21:17)	But God has revealed them *to us through His Spirit.* For the Spirit searches all things, yes, the deep things of God. For what man knows the things of a man except the spirit of the man which is in him? Even so no one knows the things of God except the Spirit of God. (1 Cor. 2:10-11)

The Triune God (The Trinity)			
Each Person	**Father**	**Son**	**Holy Spirit**
is Eternal	*The eternal God is your refuge, And underneath are the everlasting arms* (Deut. 33:27) Psalm 90:2; Isaiah 57:15	*But to the Son He says: 'Your throne, O God, is forever and ever* (Heb. 1:8) Micah 5:1-2; John 12:34	*… how much more shall the blood of Christ, who through **the eternal Spirit** offered Himself without spot to God, cleanse your conscience from dead works to serve the living God?* (Heb. 9:14) Rom. 8:11
raised Jesus from the dead	*To you first, God, having **raised up His Servant Jesus**, sent Him to bless you, in turning away every one of you from your iniquities."* (Acts 3:26) Gal. 1:1; 1 Thess. 1:8-10	*"Therefore My Father loves Me, because I lay down My life that I may take it again. No one takes it from Me, but I lay it down of Myself. I have power to lay it down, and I have power to take it again. This command I have received from My Father."* (John 10:17-18) John 2: 19-21	*But if the **Spirit of Him who raised Jesus from the dead** dwells in you, He who raised Christ from the dead will also give life to your mortal bodies through His Spirit who dwells in you.* (Rom 8:11) 1 Peter 3:18
strengthens me	*But may **the God of all grace**, who called us to His eternal glory by Christ Jesus, after you have suffered a while, perfect, establish, strengthen, and settle you.* (Peter 5:10)	*I can do all things **through Christ who strengthens me**.* (Phil. 4:13)	*For this reason I bow my knees to the Father of our Lord Jesus Christ, from whom the whole family in heaven and earth is named, that He would grant you, according to the riches of His glory, to be **strengthened with might through His Spirit in the inner man*** (Eph. 3:14-16)
searches the heart	*I, the LORD, search the heart, I test the mind, Even to give every man according to his ways, According to the fruit of his doings.* (Jer. 17:10)	*… all the churches shall know that I am He who searches the minds and hearts. And I will give to each one of you according to your works.* (Rev. 2:23)	*But God has revealed them to us through His Spirit. For the Spirit searches all things, yes, the deep things of God.* (1 Cor. 2:10)

The Triune God (The Trinity)			
Each Person	**Father**	**Son**	**Holy Spirit**
is the life giver	*And the LORD God formed man of the dust of the ground, and breathed into his nostrils the breath of life; and man became a living being.* (Gen. 2:7) *For as the Father raises the dead and gives life to them, even so the Son gives life to whom He will.* (John 5:21)	*All things were made through Him, and without Him nothing was made that was made.* (John 1:3) *For as the Father raises the dead and gives life to them, even so the Son gives life to whom He will.* (John 5:21)	who also made us sufficient as ministers of the new covenant, not of the letter but of the Spirit; for the letter kills, but the Spirit gives life. (2 Cor. 3:6) *… how will the ministry of the Spirit not be more glorious?* (2 Cor. 3:8)
speaks	*And suddenly a voice came from heaven, saying, "This is My beloved Son, in whom I am well pleased."* (Matt. 3:17)	*When He saw their faith, He said to him, "Man, your sins are forgiven you."* (Luke 5:20) *Then He said to her, "Your sins are forgiven."* (Luke 7:48)	*Then **the Spirit said** to Philip, "Go near and overtake this chariot."* (Acts 8:29) *Then the Spirit told me to go with them, doubting nothing. Moreover these six brethren accompanied me, and we entered the man's house.* (Acts 11:12) *As they ministered to the Lord and fasted, **the Holy Spirit said**, "Now separate to Me Barnabas and Saul for the work to which I have called them."* (Acts 13:2)

The Triune God (The Trinity)			
Each Person	**Father**	**Son**	**Holy Spirit**
indwells the believer	… For you are the temple of the living God. As God has said: "I will dwell in them And walk among them. I will be their God, And they shall be My people." (2 Cor. 6:16)	To them God willed to make known what are the riches of the glory of this mystery among the Gentiles: which is Christ in you, the hope of glory. (Col. 1:27)	… the Spirit of truth, whom the world cannot receive, because it neither sees Him nor knows Him; but you know Him, for He dwells with you and will be in you. (John 14:17)
has fellowship with the believer	that which we have seen and heard we declare to you, that you also may have fellowship with us; and truly our fellowship is with the Father and with His Son Jesus Christ. (1 John 1:3)	God is faithful, by whom you were called into the fellowship of His Son, Jesus Christ our Lord. (1 Cor. 1:9)	The grace of the Lord Jesus Christ, and the love of God, and the communion of the Holy Spirit be with you all. Amen. (2 Cor. 13:14) Therefore if there is any consolation in Christ, if any comfort of love, if any fellowship of the Spirit … (Phil. 2:1)
has a Will	Jesus said, "Father, if it is Your will, take this cup away from Me; nevertheless not My will, but Yours, be done." (Luke 22:42)	Jesus said, "Father, if it is Your will, take this cup away from Me; nevertheless not My will, but Yours, be done." (Luke 22:42)	But one and the same Spirit works all these things, distributing to each one individually as He wills. (1 Cor. 12:11)

The Triune God (The Trinity)			
Each Person	**Father**	**Son**	**Holy Spirit**
inspired the Prophets	"Blessed is the Lord God of Israel, For He has visited and redeemed His people, And has raised up a horn of salvation for us In the house of His servant David, As He spoke by the mouth of His holy prophets, who have been since the world began" (Luke 1:68-70)	Of this salvation the prophets have inquired and searched carefully, who prophesied of the grace that would come to you, searching what, or what manner of time, the Spirit of Christ who was in them was indicating when He testified beforehand the sufferings of Christ and the glories that would follow. (1 Peter 1:10-11)	"… this Scripture had to be fulfilled, which the Holy Spirit spoke before by the mouth of David concerning Judas, who became a guide to those who arrested Jesus" (Acts 1:16) knowing this first, that no prophecy of Scripture is of any private interpretation, for prophecy never came by the will of man, but holy men of God spoke as they were moved by the Holy Spirit. (2 Peter 1:20-21)

References:

[1] Carr, Pastor Steve. *Discipleship*, Calvary Chapel, Arroyo Grande, CA., *www.calvaryag.org, 2008*

Chapter 3, Appendix II

**Ways that other religions, cults and heretics
attack the Biblical teaching of the Trinity**

- o Jehovah's Witnesses, classic Oneness Pentecostals, and Muslims deny that God is revealed as three distinct and eternal "persons" -the Trinity. [1]
- o Mormons, Christian Scientists, and the new breed of Oneness Pentecostals believe in the Trinity, but redefine it to mean something entirely different than what the Bible says. [1]

Non-Biblical Views of Jesus [2,3]

1. Jehovah's Witnesses (Dwight D. Eisenhower, Michael Jackson)
   - o deny the deity of Jesus Christ and teach that Jesus was created
   - o claim that Jesus, in His pre-incarnate state, was the Archangel Michael.

2. Mormons (Mitt Romney, Christine Aguilera)
   - o don't believe in the Biblical doctrine of the Trinity
   - o believe that god and his goddess wife used to be people from another world (McConkie, Bruce, Mormon Doctrine, p. 192, 321, 516, 589).
   - o believe that god joined with his goddess wife and had millions of spirit children, with Jesus being the first and Lucifer (Satan) is his younger brother.
   - o believe that you and I are spirit brothers of Jesus and Lucifer (McConkie, p. 192, 589) (Doctrine & Covenants 130:22)

3. Scientology (Tom Cruise, John Travolta, Charles Manson)
   - o denies the existence of the God of the Bible, heaven, and hell
   - o denies the deity of Christ and teach Jesus was some sort of lesser god
   - o differs from biblical Christianity on every important doctrine
   - o believes that there are multiple gods and that some gods are above other gods
   - o believes that 75 million years ago, Xenu the director of a galactic confederacy, brought billions of his people to earth

4. Christian Science (Val Kilmer, Doris Day)
   - o denies that Jesus was the Christ.
   - o believes that the Christ is the "divine-idea man" and that this principle dwells within each and every one of us.
   - o teaches that God—Father-Mother of all—is wholly spiritual and that the true nature of every person is the flawless spiritual likeness of the Divine
   - o is an anti-Christian cult that points to mystical new-age spirituality as the path for physical and spiritual healing.

5. Oneness Pentecostals
    o   do not believe that God is revealed as three distinct and eternal "persons" -the Trinity
    o   believe that God is a singular spirit who manifests himself as Father, Son and Holy Spirit.
    o   baptize in the name of Jesus Christ, commonly referred to as Jesus-name baptism, rather than in the name of the Father, Son, and Holy Spirit.
    o   define salvation as 3 requirements- repentance, baptism in Jesus' name only and receipt of the Holy Spirit with the evidence of speaking in other tongues.

6. Islam (Muslims)
    o   considered Jesus to have been a Muslim and a prophet, but a prophet much lower than Muhammad
    o   does not believe that Jesus was God incarnate or the son of God
    o   does not believe that Jesus was ever crucified or resurrected, or that Jesus atoned for the sins of mankind

7. Hinduism
    o   believe Jesus was a teacher and an incarnation of their god Vishnu (Krishna)

8. Buddhism
    o   believe Jesus was a good teacher, but far less important than Buddha

---

References:

[1] Miller, Elliot, editor-in-chief of the *Christian Research Journal*

[2] Slick, Matt , President and Founder of the Christian Apologetics and Research Ministry

[3] Houdmann, S. Michael, *Got Questions? Bible Questions Answered*, Winepress Publishing, http://www.gotquestions.org/

CHAPTER FOUR
JESUS IS SAVIOR, LORD, AND CHRIST

Believe on the Lord Jesus Christ, and you will be saved, you and your household.
(Acts 16:31)

*... if you confess with your mouth the Lord Jesus and **believe in your heart** that
God has raised Him from the dead, **you will be saved**.
For **with the heart one believes** unto righteousness,
and with the mouth confession is made unto salvation.* (Romans 10:9-10)

When we say **"the Lord Jesus Christ"**, we are recognizing and confessing three
very important titles of Jesus:
- *He is The Lord*
- *He is The Savior*
- *He is The Christ*

Let's look at each one of these titles starting with: "***The Christ***"

**A. Christ is the English form of the Greek word "Christos" and of the Hebrew
word "Messiah" which both mean "the Anointed".**

1. The Messiah was the promised deliverer of the Jewish nation prophesied in the
   Hebrew Bible (the Old Testament):
   *The Messiah was the leader to come, anointed by God, descended from
   King David, who will rule the united tribes of Israel and bring the messianic
   age of world peace.*
   *Prophecy means knowledge of a future event received under inspiration
   from God.*

2. Isaiah prophesied about 700 years before Jesus was born of a virgin that the
   Messiah would be anointed by Spirit of the Lord God. (Isaiah 61)
   (Prophecy is a prediction spoken under inspiration from God.)

   *At the beginning of His ministry, Jesus quoted from the prophet Isaiah).
   And when He had opened the book, He found the place where it was written:*
   **"The Spirit of the LORD is upon Me,
   because He has annointed Me**
   *To preach the gospel to the poor;
   He has sent Me to heal the brokenhearted,
   to proclaim liberty to the captives
   And recovery of sight to the blind, to set at liberty those who are oppressed;
   To proclaim the acceptable year of the LORD."
   Then He closed the book, and gave it back to the attendant and sat down.*

And the eyes of all who were in the synagogue were fixed on Him.
And He began to say to them,
"Today this Scripture is fulfilled in your hearing."   (Luke 4: 16-21)

See more about
"the Son of Man"
in Appendix IV
of this chapter

3. Peter Confesses Jesus as the Christ.
    ... He asked His disciples, saying,
        "Who do men say that I, the Son of Man, am?"
    So they said, "Some say John the Baptist,
    some Elijah, and others Jeremiah or one of the prophets."
    He said to them, **"But who do you say that I am?"**
    Simon Peter answered and said,
        "You are the Christ, the Son of the living God."
    Jesus answered and said to him,
        "Blessed are you, Simon Bar-Jonah, for flesh and blood
        has not revealed this *to you, but My Father who is in heaven."*
                                                      (Matthew 16:13, 16)

4. John wrote in his Gospel that Jesus is "the Christ",
    And truly Jesus did many other signs in the presence of His disciples,
    which are not written in this book;
    but **these are written <u>that you may believe</u> that**
    <u>Jesus is the Christ, the Son of God,</u>
    and that believing you may have life in His name.   (John 20:30- 31**)**

    > **"... <u>that you may believe</u>"**
    > *- means that we may accept as true or real*
    > *- or to have a firm conviction of*

Let's look at His title: "**The Savior** "

B. Savior - Jesus saves and rescues His people from sin.
   "Jesus" is English for the Hebrew name **"Yeshua"** which means **"Yahweh is salvation"**

1. Jesus came down from heaven at the Father's will and by the power of the Holy Spirit.
    But while he (Joseph) thought about these things, behold, an angel of the Lord appeared to him in a dream, saying,
    "Joseph, son of David, do not be afraid to take to you Mary your wife, for that which is conceived in her is **of the Holy Spirit**. *And she will bring forth a Son, and you shall* **call His name JESUS, for He will save His people from their sins**.*"*
    So all this was done that it might be fulfilled which was spoken by the Lord through the prophet (Isaiah), *saying:*

*"Behold, the virgin shall be with child, and bear a Son, and they **shall call His name Immanuel,"** which is translated, "God with us."*

(Matthew 1:20-23; Isaiah 7:14)

Immanuel would be the presence of God with His people

2. About 800 years before Christ, the prophet Joel spoke of the Messiah who would come:

   *And it shall come to pass that **whoever calls on the name of the LORD shall be saved.***   (Joel 2: 32a)

3. The Book of Acts quotes the prophecy from Joel:

   *And it shall come to pass that **whoever calls on the name of the LORD shall be saved.***   (Acts 2:21)

   ***Salvation** is found in no one else,*
   *for there is **no other name under heaven***
   *given to men **by which we must be saved.***   (Acts 4:12)

4. What are believers saved from? We are saved from:
   a. from our former position under the punishment of God, the dominion of sin, and the power of death   (Rom. 1:18; 3:9; 5:21)
   b. from our natural condition of being mastered by the world, the flesh, and the devil   (John 8:23-24; Rom. 8:7-8; 1 John 5:19)
   c. saved from sin (…the wages of sin is death)   (Rom. 6:23)
   d. from the fears that a sinful life produces
                              (Rom. 8:15; 2 Tim.1:7; Heb. 2:14-15)
   e. from the many corrupt habits that were part of it
   For the wages of sin* is *death, but the gift of God* is *eternal life in Christ Jesus our Lord.   (Romans 6:23)
                              (Eph. 4:17-24; 1 Thess. 4:3-8)

5. Our salvation involves:
   a. Christ dying for us   (John 3:16; Romans 5:6-8)
   b. Christ living in us   (John 15:4; 17:26; Col. 1:27)
   c. Us living in Christ, united with him in His death and His risen life
                              (Rom. 6:3-10; Col. 2:12, 20; 3:1)
   d. Salvation from sin and death was wholly God's work -
   not people saving themselves with God's help.
   For it is by grace you have been saved, through faith—and this not from yourselves, it** [salvation and faith together] **is the gift of God.
                              (Eph. 2:8)

6. Believe – To be saved, we must believe that God raised Jesus Christ from the dead.

   … if you confess with your mouth the Lord Jesus and believe in your heart that God has raised Him from the dead, you will be saved.

For with the heart one believes unto righteousness, and with the mouth confession is made unto salvation.   (Romans 10:9-10)

a. The Greek word for "believe" in Romans 10:10 means:
    o to be fully convinced of
    o to trust in or to have faith in
    o to acknowledge and rely on

b. To believe means more than just a mental acceptance of truth or of a church doctrine
    o to believe is to have a personal trust that produces obedience
    o to believe includes submission and a positive confession of the Lordship of Jesus.

"For God so loved the world that He gave His only begotten Son, that whoever should not perish but have everlasting life.
For God did not send His Son into the world to condemn the world,
but that the world through Him might be saved."   (John 3:16)

But at midnight Paul and Silas were praying and singing hymns to God, and the prisoners were listening to them. Suddenly there was a great earthquake, so that the foundations of the prison were shaken; and immediately all the doors were opened and everyone's chains were loosed.
And the keeper of the prison, awaking from sleep and seeing the prison doors open, supposing the prisoners had fled, drew his sword and was about to kill himself. (He would have been executed for their escape)
But Paul called with a loud voice, saying, "Do yourself no harm, for we are all here."
*Then he called for a light, ran in, and fell down trembling before Paul and Silas. And he brought them out and said, "Sirs, **what must I do to be saved?"***

*So they said, **"Believe on the Lord Jesus Christ, and you will be saved, you and your household."***

Then they spoke the word of the Lord to him and to all who were in his house. And he took them the same hour of the night and washed their stripes. And immediately he and all his family were baptized.
*Now when he had brought them into his house, he set food before them; and he **rejoiced, having believed in God with all his household**.*
(Acts 16: 25-34)

What will you answer when someone asks you:
"What must I do to be saved."

Let's look at the His title: "*The Lord*"

C. JESUS CHRIST IS LORD

1. God the Father exalted Jesus as Lord above all:

   He (Jesus) humbled Himself and became obedient to the point of death,
      even the death of the cross.
   Therefore God also has highly exalted Him and given Him the name
      which is above every name,
   that at the name of Jesus every knee should bow, of those in heaven,
      and of those on earth, and of those under the earth,
   *and that every tongue should confess that **Jesus Christ is Lord**,*
      to the glory of God the Father.   (Philippians 2: 8b-11)

2. God the Holy Spirit declares Jesus is Lord:
   *... no one can say that **Jesus is Lord** except by the Holy Spirit.*
   (1 Corinthians 12:3b)

3. Jesus is called Lord of all in the book of Acts:
   *Then Peter opened his mouth and said: "In truth I perceive that God shows no partiality. But in every nation whoever fears Him and works righteousness is accepted by Him. The word which God sent to the children of Israel, preaching peace through **Jesus Christ—He is Lord of all.*** (Acts 10:34-36)

4. Submission – a new Master
   "Therefore, let all Israel be assured of this;
   God has made this Jesus, whom you crucified, both Lord and Christ."
   (Acts 2:36)
   a. The word "Lord" means Master - the one who calls the shots, the one who makes the decisions - the One Who has Supreme authority and unlimited power.
   b. Lordship is one of the primary messages of the Bible. Jesus is referred to as **"Lord" 92 times** in the book of Acts and **747 times** in the whole New Testament, while being referred to as "Savior" only 2 times in Acts and 24 times in the New Testament.
   c. The Bible overwhelmingly emphasizes the concept of Lordship.

5. The Lordship of Christ is essential for salvation
   a. The starting point of salvation is the acknowledgement of the Lordship of Christ.
   b. Confessing Jesus is Lord implies a submission to His Lordship in every area of our life.
   c. Someone once said, "If Jesus is not Lord of all, He is not Lord at all."

d. We do not have the option of receiving Him as Savior and not as Lord. Salvation is an all or nothing proposal.
   That if you confess with your mouth, 'Jesus is Lord,' and believe in your heart that God raised Him from the dead, you will be saved.   (Romans 10:9)

6. His Lordship in our life begins in our heart
   a. Submitting to Christ as Lord is not about following a set of religious rules and traditions.
   b. Rather, Lordship is a matter of the heart.
   c. Lordship begins as an internal decision of the heart.
   d. If it is genuine, it will eventually manifest itself in outward obedience to God's will.
      "But in your hearts set apart Christ as Lord."   (1 Peter 3:15)

7. His Lordship in our life is a lifestyle
   a. We begin our Christian life by acknowledging that Jesus is Lord.
   b. We must continue to walk under His Lordship for the rest of our lives.
   c. Lordship is not a one-time experience with God, but developing a life time walk with God.
   d. The more we know Him, the more we submit to Him.
      "So then, just as you received Christ Jesus as Lord, continue to live in Him."   (Colossians 2:6)

8. Remember in Matthew 16 that Jesus asked, *"... but Who do you say that I am?"*
   a. Take time frequently to meditate in prayer about whom you think Jesus is
   b. Then answer His question: *"Who do you say that I am?"*
   c. Then take time to know Him and to worship Him. Jesus tells us that, if we believe that Jesus Christ is our Lord, we will do as He says:

   But why do you call Me "Lord, Lord," and <u>not</u> do the things which I say?

   Whoever comes to Me, and hears My sayings and does them,
   I will show you whom he is like:
   He is like a man building a house, who dug deep and laid the foundation on the rock. And when the flood arose, the stream beat vehemently against that house, and could not shake it, for it was founded on the rock.

   But he who heard and did nothing *is like a man who built a house on the earth without a foundation, against which the stream beat vehemently; and immediately it fell. And the ruin of that house was great.*   (Luke 6:46-49)

9. A lot of people say that there are many ways to God, and some that any way is OK.   But Jesus said,
   "I am the way, the truth, and the life. No one comes to the Father except through Me."   (John 14: 6)

Chapter 4, Appendix I
17 Messianic Prophecies from Isaiah 53

These were written about 700 years before the birth of Christ.

Promise	Prophecy in Isaiah Verse	Fulfillment
Who has believed our report?	*Who has believed our report? And to whom has the arm of the LORD been revealed?* Isaiah 53:1	*But although He had done so many signs before them, they did not believe in Him, that the word of Isaiah the prophet might be fulfilled, which he spoke:* *"Lord, who has believed our report? And to whom has the arm of the LORD been revealed?"* John 12:37-38
		Romans 10:16
despised and rejected	*He is despised and rejected by men, A Man of sorrows and acquainted with grief.* Isaiah 53:3	*Then He (Jesus) answered and told them, "Indeed, Elijah is coming first and restores all things. And how is it written concerning the Son of Man, that He must suffer many things and be treated with contempt?"* Mark 9:12
		Luke 17:25, John 1:10-11, 1 Peter 2:4
He has borne our infirmities	*Surely He has borne our griefs and carried our sorrows* Isaiah 53:4	*When evening had come, they brought to Him many who were demon-possessed. And He cast out the spirits with a word, and healed all who were sick, [17] that it might be fulfilled which was spoken by Isaiah the prophet, saying: "He Himself took our infirmities and bore our sicknesses."* Matthew 8:16-17
considered smitten by God	*Yet we esteemed Him stricken, smitten by God, and afflicted.* Isaiah 53:4	*And the people stood looking on. But even the rulers with them sneered, saying, "He saved others; let Him save Himself if He is the Christ, the chosen of God."* Luke 23:35
		Galatians 3:13, Matthew 27:38-44
wounded for our transgressions	*But He was wounded for our transgressions* Isaiah 53:5	*who was delivered up because of our offenses, and was raised because of our justification.* Romans 4:25

Promise	Prophecy in Isaiah Verse	Fulfillment
We are healed by his stripes	*And by His stripes we are healed.* Isaiah 53:5	*who Himself bore our sins in His own body on the tree, that we, having died to sins, might live for righteousness—by whose stripes you were healed.* 1 Peter 2:24
Jesus was flogged	*And by His stripes we are healed.* Isaiah 53:5	*So then Pilate took Jesus and scourged Him (a whip with multiple thongs).* John 19:1
		Mark 15:15, Luke 22:63-65,
silent before His accusers	*He was oppressed and He was afflicted, Yet He opened not His mouth; He was led as a lamb to the slaughter, And as a sheep before its shearers is silent, so He opened not His mouth.* Isaiah 53:7	*(Pilate) went again into the Praetorium, and said to Jesus, "Where are You from?" But Jesus gave him no answer.* John 19:9
		Matthew 26:62-63, 27:12-14 Mark 14:60-61, 15:3-15 Acts 8:32-35
Christ died for our sins	*For He was cut off from the land of the living; For the transgressions of My people He was stricken.* Isaiah 53:8	*For I delivered to you first of all that which I also received: that Christ died for our sins according to the Scriptures* 1 Corinthians 15:3
died with the wicked	*And they made His grave with the wicked* Isaiah 53:9	*Then two robbers were crucified with Him, one on the right and another on the left.* Matthew 27:38
		Mark 15:27-28, Luke 23:32-33
buried with the rich	*But with the rich at His death* Isaiah 53:9	*… there came a rich man from Arimathea, named Joseph, who himself had also become a disciple of Jesus. …When Joseph had taken the body, he wrapped it in a clean linen cloth, and laid it in his new tomb which he had hewn out of the rock; and he rolled a large stone against the door of the tomb, and departed.* Matthew 27:57-60
		Mark 15:43-46 Luke 23:50-53 John 19:38-42
lived a sinless life	*Because He had done no violence, nor was any deceit in His mouth.* Isaiah 53:9	*… Who committed no sin, nor was deceit found in His mouth* 1 Peter 2:22

Promise	Prophecy in Isaiah Verse	Fulfillment
Jesus was an offering for sin	*Yet it pleased the LORD to bruise Him; He has put Him to grief. When You make His soul an offering for sin* Isaiah 53:10	*For I delivered to you first of all that which I also received: that Christ died for our sins according to the Scriptures* 1 Corinthians 15:3
		Hebrews 10:12-14
He would justify many	*By His knowledge My righteous Servant shall justify many, For He shall bear their iniquities.* Isaiah 53:11	*Therefore let it be known to you, brethren, that through this Man is preached to you the forgiveness of sins; and by Him everyone who believes is justified from all things from which you could not be justified by the law of Moses.* Acts 13:38-39
		Romans 5:17-19
He will be great	*Therefore I will divide Him a portion with the great* Isaiah 53:12	*And Jesus came and spoke to them, saying, "All authority has been given to Me in heaven and on earth.* Matthew 28:18
		Luke 24:27
numbered with transgressors	*And He was numbered with the transgressors, and He bore the sin of many,* Isaiah 53:12	*Then two robbers were crucified with Him, one on the right and another on the left.* Matthew 27:38
		Mark 15:27-28, Luke 23:32-33
made intercession for sinners	*And made intercession for the transgressors.* Isaiah 53:12	*Then Jesus said, "Father, forgive them, for they do not know what they do."* Luke 23:34
		Luke 23:39-43, Romans 8:34

Chapter 4, Appendix II
12 Prophecies from Psalm 22 about the crucifixion of Jesus

These were written about <u>1,000 years before</u> the birth of Christ.

Promise	Prophecy in Psalm Verse	Fulfillment
the forsaken Christ	*My God, My God, why have You forsaken Me?* Psalm 22:1	*And about the ninth hour Jesus cried out with a loud voice, saying, "Eli, Eli, lama sabachthani?" that is, "My God, My God, why have You forsaken Me?"* Matthew 27:46
		Mark 15:34
verbally abused by men	*But I am a worm, and no man; A reproach of men, and despised by the people. All those who see Me ridicule Me;* Psalm 22:6-7	*Then they spat in His face and beat Him; and others struck Him with the palms of their hands, saying, "Prophesy to us, Christ! Who is the one who struck You?"* *Then the soldiers of the governor took Jesus into the Praetorium and gathered the whole garrison around Him. And they stripped Him and put a scarlet robe on Him. When they had twisted a crown of thorns, they put it on His head, and a reed in His right hand. And they bowed the knee before Him and mocked Him, saying, "Hail, King of the Jews!" Then they spat on Him, and took the reed and struck Him on the head. And when they had mocked Him, they took the robe off Him, put His own clothes on Him, and led Him away to be crucified.* Matthew 26:67-68, 27:27-31
surrounded by enemies	*Many bulls have surrounded Me; Strong bulls of Bashan have encircled Me.* Psalm 22:12	

Promise	Prophecy in Psalm Verse	Fulfillment
His trust in God ridiculed	*They shoot out the lip, they shake the head, saying,* "*He trusted in the LORD, let Him rescue Him; Let Him deliver Him, since He delights in Him!*" Psalm 22:8	*And those who passed by blasphemed Him, wagging their heads and saying, "You who destroy the temple and build it in three days, save Yourself! If You are the Son of God, come down from the cross." Likewise the chief priests also, mocking with the scribes and elders, said, "He saved others; Himself He cannot save. If He is the King of Israel, let Him now come down from the cross, and we will believe Him. He trusted in God; let Him deliver Him now if He will have Him; for He said, 'I am the Son of God.'" Even the robbers who were crucified with Him reviled Him with the same thing.* Matthew 27:39-44
		Mark 15:29-32, Luke 23:35, 39
physically weakened	*I am poured out like water, And all My bones are out of joint; My heart is like wax; It has melted within Me. My strength is dried up like a potsherd,* Psalm 22:14-15	*Now as they came out, they found a man of Cyrene, Simon by name. Him they compelled to bear His cross.* Matthew 27:32
		Mark 15:21, Luke 23:26
thirsty	*And My tongue clings to My jaws; You have brought Me to the dust of death* Psalm 22:15	*After this, Jesus, knowing that all things were now accomplished, that the Scripture might be fulfilled, said, "I thirst!"* John 19:28
hands and feet pierced	*They pierced My hands and My feet* Psalm 22:16	*When He had said this, He showed them His hands and His side. Then the disciples were glad when they saw the Lord.* John 20:20, 25
stared at by the people	*They look and stare at Me.* Psalm 22:17	*Then many of the Jews read this title, for the place where Jesus was crucified was near the city; and it was written in Hebrew, Greek, and Latin.* John 19:20
		Matthew 27:55-56; Luke 23:35, 48-49

Promise	Prophecy in Psalm Verse	Fulfillment
bones not broken	*I can count all My bones.* Psalm 22:17	*Then the soldiers came and broke the legs of the first and of the other who was crucified with Him. But when they came to Jesus and saw that He was already dead, they did not break His legs.. For these things were done that the Scripture should be fulfilled, "Not one of His bones shall be broken.* John 19: 32, 33, 36
lots cast for His clothing	*They divide My garments among them, And for My clothing they cast lots.* Psalm 22:18	*Then they crucified Him, and divided His garments, casting lots, that it might be fulfilled which was spoken by the prophet: "They divided My garments among them, And for My clothing they cast lots."* Matthew 27:35
		Mark 15:24, Luke 23:34, John 19:23-24
God heard His prayers	*You have answered Me.* *For He has not despised nor abhorred the affliction of the afflicted; Nor has He hidden His face from; But when He cried to Him, He heard.* Psalm 22:21, 24	*Who, in the days of His flesh, when He had offered up prayers and supplications, with vehement cries and tears to Him who was able to save Him from death, and was heard because of His godly fear, though He was a Son, yet He learned obedience by the things which He suffered.* Hebrews 5:7-8

References:

[1] Palmer, Ken, *www.lifeofchrist.com*

Chapter 4, Appendix III
19 Messianic Prophecies from Various Psalms
These verses from Psalms <u>were fulfilled</u> in the New Testament Verses noted.

Portrayal	Prophecy in Psalm Verse	Fulfillment
The Son of God	*"I will declare the decree: The LORD has said to Me, 'You are My Son, Today I have begotten You."* Psalm 2: 7	*And suddenly a voice came from heaven, saying, "This is My beloved Son, in whom I am well pleased."* Matthew 3: 17
praised by children	*Out of the mouth of babes and nursing infants You have ordained strength,* Psalm 8: 2	*But when the chief priests and scribes saw the wonderful things that He did, and the children crying out in the temple and saying, "Hosanna to the Son of David!" they were indignant* Matthew 21: 15, 16
Ruler of all	*You have made him to have dominion over the works of Your hands; You have put all things under his feet* Psalm 8: 6	*You have put all things in subjection under his feet. For in that He put all in subjection under him, He left nothing that is not put under him. But now we do not yet see all things put under him.* Hebrews 2: 8
rises from the dead	*For You will not leave my soul in Sheol, Nor will You allow Your Holy One to see corruption.* Psalm 16: 10	*And go quickly and tell His disciples that He is risen from the dead, and indeed He is going before you into Galilee; there you will see Him. Behold, I have told you."* Matthew 28: 7
bones unbroken	*He guards all his bones; Not one of them is broken.* Psalm 34: 20	*Then the soldiers came and broke the legs of the first and of the other who was crucified with Him. But when they came to Jesus and saw that He was already dead, they did not break His legs. For these things were done that the Scripture should be fulfilled, "Not one of His bones shall be broken.* John 19: 32, 33, 36

Portrayal	Prophecy in Psalm Verse	Fulfillment
accused by false witnesses	*Fierce witnesses rise up; They ask me things that I do not know* Psalm 35: 11	*Then some rose up and bore false witness against Him* Mark 14: 57
hated without cause	*Let them not rejoice over me who are wrongfully my enemies; Nor let them wink with the eye who hate me without a cause.* Psalm 35: 19	*But this happened that the word might be fulfilled which is written in their law, 'They hated Me without a cause.'* John 15: 25
delights in God's will	*Then I said, "Behold, I come; In the scroll of the book it is written of me."* Psalm 40: 7, 8	*Then I said, 'Behold, I have come— In the volume of the book it is written of Me— To do Your will, O God.'"* Hebrews 10: 7
betrayed by a friend	*Even my own familiar friend in whom I trusted, who ate my bread, has lifted up his heel against me.* Psalm 41: 9	*And while He was still speaking, behold, a multitude; and he who was called Judas, one of the twelve, went before them and drew near to Jesus to kiss Him.* Luke 22: 47
The eternal King	*Your throne, O God, is forever and ever; A scepter of righteousness is the scepter of Your kingdom.* Psalm 45: 6	*But to the Son He says: "Your throne, O God, is forever and ever; A scepter of righteousness is the scepter of Your kingdom."* Hebrews 1: 8
Ascends to heaven	*You have ascended on high, You have led captivity captive; You have received gifts among men, Even from the rebellious, That the LORD God might dwell there.* Psalm 68: 18	*As he (Saul) journeyed he came near Damascus, and suddenly a light shone around him from heaven. [4] Then he fell to the ground, and heard a voice saying to him, "Saul, Saul, why are you persecuting Me?" And he said, "Who are You, Lord?" Then the Lord said, "I am Jesus, whom you are persecuting. It is hard for you to kick against the goads."* Acts 9: 3-5

Portrayal	Prophecy in Psalm Verse	Fulfillment
zealous for God's house	*Because zeal for Your house has eaten me up (consumed me), and the reproaches of those who reproach You have fallen on me.* Psalm 69: 9	*Then His disciples remembered that it was written, "Zeal for Your house has eaten Me up (consumed me)."* John 2: 17
given vinegar and gall	*They also gave me gall for my food, and for my thirst they gave me vinegar to drink.* Psalm 69: 21	*they gave Him sour wine mingled with gall to drink. But when He had tasted it, He would not drink.* Matthew 27: 34
prays for His enemies	*In return for my love they are my accusers, But I give myself to prayer.* Psalm 109: 4	*Then Jesus said, "Father, forgive them, for they do not know what they do." And they divided His garments and cast lots.* Luke 23: 34
His betrayer replaced	*Let his days be few, And let another take his office.* Psalm 109: 8	*"For it is written in the Book of Psalms: 'Let his dwelling place be desolate, And let no one live in it'; and, 'Let another take his office.'* Acts 1: 20
rules over His enemies	*The LORD said to my Lord, "Sit at My right hand, Till I make Your enemies Your footstool."* Psalm 110: 1	*'The LORD said to my Lord, "Sit at My right hand, Till I make Your enemies Your footstool"'* Matthew 22: 44
A priest forever	*The LORD has sworn and will not relent, "You are a priest forever according to the order of Melchizedek."* Psalm 110: 4	*As He also says in another place: "You are a priest forever According to the order of Melchizedek"* Hebrews 5: 6
The chief stone of God's building	*The stone which the builders rejected has become the chief cornerstone.* Psalm 118: 22	*Jesus said to them, "Have you never read in the Scriptures: 'The stone which the builders rejected has become the chief cornerstone. This was the LORD's doing, And it is marvelous in our eyes'"?* Matthew 21: 42

Portrayal	Prophecy in Psalm Verse	Fulfillment
comes in the name of the Lord	*Blessed is he who comes in the name of the LORD! We have blessed you from the house of the LORD.* Psalm 118: 26	*Then the multitudes who went before and those who followed cried out, saying: "Hosanna to the Son of David! Blessed is He who comes in the name of the LORD! Hosanna in the highest!"* Matthew 21: 9

References:

New King James Version of the Bible, Thomas Nelson Inc., 1982

Chapter 4, Appendix IV
The Appearances of the Risen Christ Jesus

Some of the appearances of the Lord Jesus that occurred for 40 days after
His death, burial and resurrection, and some just prior to His ascension to heaven.

Jesus appeared	Portions of the Scriptures for when Jesus appeared after His death, burial and resurrection
in or around Jerusalem to Mary Magdalene and to another Mary	*Now when He rose early on the first day of the week, He appeared first to Mary Magdalene, out of whom He had cast seven demons. She went and told those who had been with Him, as they mourned and wept.* (Mark 16:9-10)
	But Mary stood outside by the tomb weeping, and as she wept she stooped down and looked into the tomb. And she saw two angels in white sitting, one at the head and the other at the feet, where the body of Jesus had lain. Then they said to her, "Woman, why are you weeping?" *She said to them, "Because they have taken away my Lord, and I do not know where they have laid Him."* *Now when she had said this, she turned around and saw Jesus standing there, and did not know that it was Jesus. Jesus said to her, "Woman, why are you weeping? Whom are you seeking?"* *She, supposing Him to be the gardener, said to Him, "Sir, if You have carried Him away, tell me where You have laid Him, and I will take Him away."* *Jesus said to her, "Mary!"* *She turned and said to Him, "Rabboni!" (which is to say, Teacher).* (John 20:11-16)
Mary Magdalene and Mary worship the risen Lord	*So they went out quickly from the tomb with fear and great joy, and ran to bring His disciples word. And as they went to tell His disciples behold, Jesus met them, saying, "Rejoice!" So they came and held Him by the feet and worshiped Him. Then Jesus said to them, "Do not be afraid. Go and tell My brethren to go to Galilee, and there they will see Me."* (Matt. 28:8-10)
to Peter	*So they rose up that very hour and returned to Jerusalem, and found the eleven and those who were with them gathered together, saying, "The Lord is risen indeed, and has appeared to Simon!"* (Luke 24:33-34)
to ten disciples	*Now as they said these things, Jesus Himself stood in the midst of them, and said to them, "Peace to you." But they were terrified and frightened, and supposed they had seen a spirit. And He said to them, "Why are you troubled? And why do doubts arise in your hearts? Behold My hands and My feet, that it is I Myself. Handle Me and see, for a spirit does not have flesh and bones as you see I have."* (Luke 24:36-39)

to two of the disciples on the road to Emmaus	*Now behold, two of them were traveling that same day to a village called Emmaus, which was seven miles from Jerusalem. And they talked together of all these things which had happened. So it was, while they conversed and reasoned, that Jesus Himself drew near and went with them. But their eyes were restrained, so that they did not know Him.* *Now it came to pass, as He sat at the table with them, that He took bread, blessed and broke it, and gave it to them. Then their eyes were opened and they knew Him; and He vanished from their sight. And they said to one another, "Did not our heart burn within us while He talked with us on the road, and while He opened the Scriptures to us?" So they rose up that very hour and returned to Jerusalem, and found the eleven and those who were with them gathered together* (Luke 24:13-33)
to the Eleven	(The Great Commission) *Later He appeared to the eleven as they sat at the table; and He rebuked their unbelief and hardness of heart, because they did not believe those who had seen Him after He had risen. And He said to them, "Go into all the world and preach the gospel to every creature. He who believes and is baptized will be saved; but he who does not believe will be condemned. And these signs will follow those who believe: In My name they will cast out demons; they will speak with new tongues; they will take up serpents; and if they drink anything deadly, it will by no means hurt them; they will lay hands on the sick, and they will recover."* (Mark 16:14-19)
	And after eight days His disciples were again inside, and Thomas with them. Jesus came, the doors being shut, and stood in the midst, and said, "Peace to you!" Then He said to Thomas, "Reach your finger here, and look at My hands; and reach your hand here, and put it into My side. Do not be unbelieving, but believing." *And Thomas answered and said to Him, "My Lord and my God!"* *Jesus said to him, "Thomas, because you have seen Me, you have believed. Blessed are those who have not seen and yet have believed."* (John 20:26-29)
in Galilee	*Then the eleven disciples went away into Galilee, to the mountain which Jesus had appointed for them. When they saw Him, they worshiped Him; but some doubted. And Jesus came and spoke to them, saying, "All authority has been given to Me in heaven and on earth. Go therefore and make disciples of all the nations, baptizing them in the name of the Father and of the Son and of the Holy Spirit, teaching them to observe all things that I have commanded you; and lo, I am with you always, even to the end of the age." Amen.* (Matt. 28:16-20)
	After these things Jesus showed Himself again to the disciples at the Sea of Tiberias, and in this way He showed Himself: Simon Peter, Thomas called the Twin, Nathanael of Cana in Galilee, the sons of Zebedee, and two others of His disciples were together. *This is now the third time Jesus showed Himself to His disciples after He was raised from the dead.* (John 21:1-2,14)

to five hundred people	*After that He was seen by over five hundred brethren at once, of whom the greater part remain to the present, but some have fallen asleep.* (1 Cor. 15:6)
to James and the apostles	*After that He was seen by James, then by all the apostles.* (1 Cor. 15:7)
to Paul on the road to Damascus	*As he (Paul) journeyed he came near Damascus, and suddenly a light shone around him from heaven. Then he fell to the ground, and heard a voice saying to him, "Saul, Saul, why are you persecuting Me?"* *And he said, "Who are You, Lord?"* *Then the Lord said, "I am Jesus, whom you are persecuting."* (Acts 9:3-5a)
	Now the Lord spoke to Paul in the night by a vision, "Do not be afraid, but speak, and do not keep silent; for I am with you, and no one will attack you to hurt you; for I have many people in this city." (Acts 18:9-10)
	But the following night the Lord stood by him (Paul) and said, "Be of good cheer, Paul; for as you have testified for Me in Jerusalem, so you must also bear witness at Rome." (Acts 23:11)
	(To King Agrippa Paul recalls his Damascus conversion to the Lord Jesus) *So I said, 'Who are You, Lord?' And He said, 'I am Jesus, whom you are persecuting. But rise and stand on your feet; for I have appeared to you for this purpose, to make you a minister and a witness both of the things which you have seen and of the things which I will yet reveal to you. I will deliver you from the Jewish people, as well as from the Gentiles, to whom I now send you, to open their eyes, in order to turn them from darkness to light, and from the power of Satan to God, that they may receive forgiveness of sins and an inheritance among those who are sanctified by faith in Me.'* (Acts 26:15-18)
	For I delivered to you first of all that which I also received: that Christ died for our sins according to the Scriptures, and that He was buried, and that He rose again the third day according to the Scriptures, and that He was seen by Cephas(Peter), then by the twelve. After that He was seen by over five hundred brethren at once, of whom the greater part remain to the present, but some have fallen asleep. After that He was seen by James, then by all the apostles. Then last of all He was seen by me also, as by one born out of due time. (1 Cor. 15:3-8)

at His ascension	*So then, after the Lord had spoken to them, He was received up into heaven, and sat down at the right hand of God. And they went out and preached everywhere, the Lord working with them and confirming the word through the accompanying signs. Amen.* (Mark 16:19,20)
	Behold, I send the Promise of My Father upon you; but tarry in the city of Jerusalem until you are endued with power from on high." *And He led them out as far as Bethany, and He lifted up His hands and blessed them. Now it came to pass, while He blessed them, that He was parted from them and carried up into heaven. And they worshiped Him, and returned to Jerusalem with great joy, and were continually in the temple praising and blessing God. Amen.* (Luke 24:50-53)
	And being assembled together with them, He commanded them not to depart from Jerusalem, but to wait for the Promise of the Father, "which," He said, "you have heard from Me; for John truly baptized with water, but you shall be baptized with the Holy Spirit not many days from now." *Now when He had spoken these things, while they watched, He was taken up, and a cloud received Him out of their sight. And while they looked steadfastly toward heaven as He went up, behold, two men stood by them in white apparel, who also said, "Men of Galilee, why do you stand gazing up into heaven? This same Jesus, who was taken up from you into heaven, will so come in like manner as you saw Him go into heaven."* (Acts 1:4-5,9-12)
to John on the Island of Patmos	*Then I turned to see the voice that spoke with me. And having turned I saw seven golden lampstands, and in the midst of the seven lampstands* **One like the Son of Man**, *clothed with a garment down to the feet and girded about the chest with a golden band. His head and hair were white like wool, as white as snow, and His eyes like a flame of fire; His feet were like fine brass, as if refined in a furnace, and His voice as the sound of many waters; He had in His right hand seven stars, out of His mouth went a sharp two-edged sword, and His countenance was like the sun shining in its strength. And when I saw Him, I fell at His feet as dead. But He laid His right hand on me, saying to me, "Do not be afraid; I am the First and the Last. I am He who lives, and was dead, and behold, I am alive forevermore. Amen. And I have the keys of Hades and of Death.* (Rev 1: 12-18)

Chapter 4, Appendix V
The Prophet Daniel's Vision of Jesus

This prophecy in the book of Daniel was written about 600 years before the birth of Jesus Christ.

I was watching in the night visions,
and behold, **One** *like the Son of Man,*
coming with the clouds of heaven!

He came to **the Ancient of Days,**
and they brought Him near before Him.

Then **to Him was given** *dominion and glory and a kingdom,*
That **all peoples, nations, and languages should serve Him**.

His dominion *is* **an everlasting dominion,** *which* **shall not pass away,**
and **His kingdom** *the one which* **shall not be destroyed**.   (Daniel 7: 13-14)

Dominion – supreme authority

Kingdom – the eternal Kingship of God;

        the realm in which God's will is fulfilled

Jesus said for us to …

"Seek first the kingdom of God" and everything else would be added unto us.

CHAPTER FIVE
THE HOLY SPIRIT WAS SENT BY JESUS AND THE FATHER

The Holy Spirit is sent by Jesus the Son and by God the Father
to dwell in, to empower, to teach, to guide, and to comfort believers.

> *Jesus told His disciples, "Nevertheless, I tell you the truth.*
> *It is to your own advantage that I go away;*
> *For if I do not go away, the Helper will not come to you;*
> *But if I depart, I will send Him to you."*   (John 16:7)

A. Before He was arrested and crucified, Jesus promised that He would send the Holy Spirit to us.

(See verse John 16:7 above in the shaded box)

1. The word **Helper** is translated from the Greek word **parakletos** [1] which means
   a. One called to our side, called to our aid
   b. One who helps us and comforts us (a strengthening presence)
   c. One who advises and encourages us, and who is our ally
   d. One who pleads our cause, an intercessor
   e. of Jesus, God the Son, exalted at God the Father's right hand, pleading with God the Father for the pardon of our sins
   f. of God the Holy Spirit to take the place of Christ after his ascension to the Father, to give the apostles divine strength needed to enable them to undergo trials and persecutions on behalf of the divine kingdom

2. Remember that the Holy Spirit Himself is God together with the Father and the Son   (Acts 5: 3-4 Ananias lied to God the Holy Spirit).

B. Jesus promised He would pray for the Father to send us the Holy Spirit

After Jesus predicted to the disciples about His death on the cross, He told them:
> *If you love me, (you will) keep my commandments.*
> *And **I will pray the Father, and He shall give you another Helper,***
> ***so that He may be with you forever, the Spirit of Truth,***
> *whom the world cannot receive because it does not see Him nor know Him.*
> ***But you know Him, for He dwells with you and shall be in you.***
>
> (John 14: 15-17)

1. From the verse above, we see that God wants us **"to know Him"**.

2. The Holy Spirit dwells *"with us"* and *"inside us"*

3. *"another Helper"* points to the fact that Jesus Himself was the first Helper; also means a **Comforter**, *a* **Consoler**

4. and Jesus promised that another One like Jesus, after He is gone, will carry on the teaching and testimony that Jesus started   (John 16: 6-7)

5. Holy Spirit ministry (Paraclete ministry described in section A.1 on the previous page) is *personal, relational ministry to each of us*

6. The Holy Spirit witnesses to us about the Lord Jesus Christ and glorifies Jesus by showing us and revealing to us Who Jesus is   (John 16:7-15)

7. The central ministry of the Holy Spirit is making us aware of who and what we are in Jesus   (Rom. 8:15-17; Gal. 4:6)

8. **All of God's work in us – when He touches our hearts, our characters, and our conduct – is done by the Holy Spirit**

C. INDWELL – Jesus said to be filled with the Holy Spirit

1. To have the victory over our sin nature and our addictive behaviors, we must be continually filled and controlled by the Holy Spirit by submitting to Him and by trusting Him.

2. When Jesus first appeared to the disciples after His resurrection, He said: *"Receive the Holy Spirit"*   (John 20:22)

3. This is where the disciples were born again and **where the Holy Spirit came to indwell them - to live in them**.

4. **God gave the Holy Spirit to dwell in us to help us.**

5. After Jesus breathed on the disciples to receive the Holy Spirit, Jesus then told them to wait in Jerusalem until they **"are endued** *(clothed or equipped)* **with power from on high"** (baptized with the Holy Spirit)
            (Luke 24:44-53 ; Acts 1:1-11)

6. The word **baptize** means to cover completely, to dip, to engulf, or to overwhelm. God wants to completely engulf you and overwhelm you with His power so that you will <u>not</u> be overwhelmed by the power of your sin nature.

D. Being continually filled with the Holy Spirit [3]

1. Being filled with the Holy Spirit is <u>not a once-for-all experience</u>.
   There are many fillings, as is made clear in Ephesians 5:18.

   > *See then that you walk circumspectly, not as fools but as wise,*
   > *redeeming the time, because the days are evil.*
   > *Therefore do not be unwise, but understand what the will of the Lord is.*
   > *And do not be drunk with wine, in which is dissipation;*
   > > *but **be filled with the Spirit**, speaking to one another in psalms and hymns*
   > > *and spiritual songs, singing and making melody in your heart to the Lord,*
   > *giving thanks always for all things to God the Father*
   > > *in the name of our Lord Jesus Christ,*
   > *submitting to one another in the fear of God.*   (Ephesians 5:15-21)

2. In the original Greek, "***be filled with the Spirit***" means "***keep on being filled constantly and continually***."   Living a godly life is a vital part of this process.

3. Life Application- The Spirit-Filled Life is an obedient and abiding life. It can be experienced daily as you:
   a. Love God with all of your heart
   b. Spend time daily in prayer and Bible study
   c. Obey God's commands
   d. Witness for Christ

4. Questions for us as Spirit Filled believers

   a. How is the Holy Spirit's fullness and power evident in your life?
   b. List any areas of your life in which the Holy Spirit **is not in control**.
   c. List the areas where the Holy Spirit **is in control**.
   d. What **practical steps** will you take this week to give the Holy Spirit full control of those areas that you have not surrendered to Him?
   e. Have you **realized a victory today** over a sin you confessed yesterday? Describe.

E. EMPOWER – The Holy Spirit empowers us to be Jesus' witness

1. We just read that Jesus told His disciples to wait in Jerusalem to be **baptized with the Holy Spirit.**

2. Jesus told his disciples to wait, because He knew they would <u>not be effective without the baptism of the Holy Spirit</u>.

3. The baptism of the Holy Spirit:
   a. turned fearful disciples into bold witnesses.
   b. turned powerless followers into miracle working servants. (Acts 4:18 - Peter and John - healing of man lame from birth – 5,000 saved that day)
   c. turned students with dulled understanding into prophetic ministers.
   d. The Lord Jesus gave these accounts in His Word to us and gave His **promise that the Holy Spirit would also turn us into the same Spirit-filled believers as the first Christians.**

4. Jesus is quoted in the book of Acts <u>telling us why we need to receive the Holy Spirit</u>:
   "It is not for you to know times or seasons which the Father
   has put in His own authority.
   *But **you shall receive power when the Holy Spirit has come upon you;** *
   *** and you shall be witnesses to Me** in Jerusalem, and in all Judea and*
   Samaria, and to the end of the earth."   (Acts 1: 7-8)

5. Peter is quoted in the book of Acts (healing of man lame from birth):
   "Now, Lord, look on their threats,
   * and **grant to Your servants that with all boldness they may speak Your word,** *
   by stretching out Your hand to heal, and that signs and wonders
   may be done through the name of Your holy Servant Jesus."
   And when they had prayed, the place where they were
   assembled together was shaken;
   and they were all filled with the Holy Spirit,
   and they spoke the word of God with boldness.   (Acts 4: 29-31)

F. TEACH – The Holy Spirit teaches us
Jesus said:
"Now when they bring you to the synagogues and magistrates and authorities,
* do not worry about how or what you should answer, or what you should say.*
*For **the Holy Spirit will teach you** in that very hour what you ought to say"*
                                                            (Luke 12: 11-12)
But the Helper, the Holy Spirit, whom the Father will send in My name,
   He will teach you all things,
and bring to your remembrance all things that I said to you.   (John 14:26)

G. COMFORT – The Holy Spirit comforts us
Then the churches throughout all Judea, Galilee, and Samaria had peace and were
edified (built up). And walking in the fear of the Lord and
in the comfort of the Holy Spirit, they were multiplied.   (Acts 9:31)

H. GUIDE - The Holy Spirit guides us

1. Jesus always refers to the Holy Spirit as a living person of the Trinity, together with Jesus the Son and God the Father.

2. Look at the words of Jesus in John 16- one example of how Jesus always refers to the Holy Spirit as "He" not "It": (everywhere it says "He" you can say "the Holy Spirit")

> *However, when **He**, the Spirit of truth, has come,*
> ***He** will guide you into all truth;*
> *   for **He** will not speak on **His** own authority,*
> *   but whatever **He** hears **He** will speak;*
> *   and **He** will tell you things to come.*
> ***He** will glorify Me,*
> *   for **He** will take of what is Mine and declare it to you.*
> *All things that the Father has are Mine.*
> *Therefore I said that **He** will take of Mine and declare it to you.*
>
> (John 16: 13-15)

> "whatever He hears"-
> The Holy Spirit will hear
> God the Son and
> declare it to us

I. Jesus said to <u>not be afraid</u> to receive the Holy Spirit

1. Have you ever been afraid to ask God the Father to fill you with the Holy Spirit?
   a. **You don't have to be afraid**. Look at the words of Jesus in Luke 11.
   b. After the Lord Jesus taught them how to pray "the Lord's Prayer" to the Father (Luke 11: 1-2), Jesus told them how to receive the Holy Spirit.

2. **Jesus taught them not to fear the Gift of the Holy Spirit from the Father**, because God would <u>not</u> give them something harmful when they ask Him. Jesus said:

> *"So I say to you, **ask**, and it will be given to you;*
> ***seek**, and you will find; **knock**, and it will be opened to you.*
> *For everyone who asks receives, and he who seeks finds,*
> *   and to him who knocks it will be opened.*
> *If a son asks for bread from any father among you, will he give him a stone?*
> *Or if he asks for a fish, will he give him a serpent instead of a fish?*
> *   Or if he asks for an egg, will he offer him a scorpion?*
>
> *If you then, being evil, know how to give good gifts to your children,*
> *   how much more will your heavenly Father*
> *   give the Holy Spirit to those who ask Him!"*   (Luke 11: 9-13)

> "ask...seek...
> knock" in Greek
> means to ask,
> seek, knock
> continually

3. Paul asked the believers in Ephesus in the book of Acts:

> *"Did you receive the Holy Spirit when you believed?"*
>   *So they said to him,*
> *"We have not so much as heard whether there is a Holy Spirit."*
>   *And he said to them, "Into what then were you baptized?"*
> *So they said, "Into John's baptism."*
>   *Then Paul said, "John indeed baptized with a baptism of repentance, saying to the people that they should believe on Him who would come after him, that is, on Christ Jesus."*
>   *When they heard this, they were baptized in the name of the Lord Jesus. And when Paul had laid hands on them, the Holy Spirit came upon them, and they spoke with tongues and prophesied.*   (Acts 19: 2-6)

4. If you have not asked for this gift, begin to seek and to ask God for the gift of Holy Spirit. If you need help, ask one of the pastors or leadership of the church for assistance.

References:

[1] Packer, J.I., *Concise Theology: A Guide to Historic Christian Beliefs*, 1993

[2] Carr, Pastor Steve, *Discipleship Series*, Calvary Chapel, Arroyo Grande, CA, *http://calvaryag.org/index.php?option=com_content&view=article&id=32&Itemid=43*

[3] from *The 10 Basic Steps Toward Christian Maturity*, by Bill Bright, co-founder of Campus Crusade for Christ

Chapter 5, Appendix I
Fellowship with the Father, the Son, and the Holy Spirit [1]

A. We are to have fellowship with the Father and with His Son Jesus Christ:

> *... that which we have seen and heard we declare to you,*
> *that you also may have fellowship with us;*
> *and truly our fellowship is with the Father and with His Son Jesus Christ.*
>
> (1 John 1: 3)

B. We are to have fellowship with the Holy Spirit:

> *The grace of the Lord Jesus Christ, and the love of God,*
> *and the communion (fellowship) of the Holy Spirit be with you all. Amen.*
>
> (2 Cor. 13: 14)

C. The word *communion*, also translated *fellowship*, is the word *koinonia* in the original Greek.

The word *fellowship* was <u>never used</u> to describe man's relationship to God before the Holy Spirit came on the day of Pentecost to indwell the church.

Before then, *fellowship* was used to describe corporations, partners in a law firm, and the most intimate of marriage relationships.

D. *Fellowship* is <u>primarily an action word</u>, and it is used 19 times in the New Testament.

Other New Testament synonyms for the word *fellowship* are "a sharer in a common enterprise" (*hetairos*) and "a fellow-worker" (*sunergos*).

E. Fellowship is <u>not just being together</u>.

It is our partnership and intimate reactive relationship with God the Father, with Jesus Christ the Son of God, and with God the Holy Spirit to actively do God's will.

And fellowship is our relationship with other believers in co-participation with one another and with God to accomplish God's will on earth.

F. Before He left and sent the Holy Spirit, the Lord Jesus told us what to do.

After Jesus arose from the dead, He said:
"All authority has been given to Me in heaven and on earth."
Then He said *"Go therefore"* (because of that authority given to Him)
"and make disciples of all the nations,
baptizing them in the name of the Father and of the Son and of the Holy Spirit,
teaching them to observe all things that I have commanded you;
and lo, I am with you always, even to the end of the age." Amen
(Matt 28: 18-20)

References:

[1] Gilliam, Bob, *The Importance of Fellowship in a New Testament Church,* from the Series: *The Measure of a New Testament Church*, *http://bible.org/seriespage/importance-fellowship-new-testament-church*

Chapter 5, Appendix II
Walking in the Power of the Holy Spirit

A. The Holy Spirit living in us is the greatest blessing God could ever give to any person.

1. The Holy Spirit is more than a power or influence within us.
2. The Holy Spirit is God Himself Who has come to live in us and through us.
3. Failure to recognize, to seek, and to yield to the Holy Spirit is the reason why Christians struggle with sin in their lives.
4. The Holy Spirit is the only person who can enable us to live the Christian life, and the only one who can control our strong desires and drives. Paul said,
5. *"Walk in the Spirit, and you shall not fulfill the lust of the flesh"*   (Gal. 5:16)
6. Therefore, it is very important that we surrender our life fully to the Spirit's control.

B. What steps can we take to apply these truths?

1. The next time you sense your sinful desires beginning to control you, stop and make a choice.
   a. Choose to resist these desires and reckon yourself dead to sin. (Rom. 6:11)
   b. Choose at that moment to yield to God.   (Rom. 6:12-13)
2. Acknowledge your desires that cause you to sin
   a. Confess your sin and receive His forgiveness.   (1 John 1:9)
   b. Ask the Holy Spirit to come and fill you to overflowing.
                                                          (Luke 11:13 , Eph. 5:18)
   c. Begin immediately to thank Him for answering your prayer and filling you.
                                                                        (Phil. 4:6)
   d. Wait upon the Holy Spirit completely expecting Him to work in you.
   e. Believe that the Holy Spirit is doing just what He promised.   (Is. 40:31)
   f. If later in the day, you sense the same old desires coming back, surrender yourself to God and ask Him to fill you again with the Holy Spirit.
   g. The Holy Spirit is your answer to a victorious Christian life.

   *Or do you not know that **your body is the temple of the Holy Spirit***
       Who is in you,
       *Whom you have from God, and **you are not your own?***
   *For you were **bought at a price;***
       therefore glorify God in your body and in your spirit, which are God's.
                                                                  (1 Cor. 6: 19-20)

*For those **who live according to the flesh** set their minds on the things of the flesh,*

*but those **who live according to the Spirit**, the things of the Spirit.*
So then, those who are in the flesh cannot please God.
*But you are not in the flesh but in the Spirit, if indeed **the Spirit of God dwells in you**.*

*Now if anyone does not **have the Spirit of Christ**, he is not His.*
***And if Christ is in you**, the body is dead because of sin,*

but the Spirit is life because of righteousness.
*But if **the Spirit of Him who raised Jesus from the dead dwells in you**,*
He who raised Christ from the dead will also give life to your mortal bodies

through His Spirit who dwells in you.   (Rom. 8: 1-11)

Chapter 5, Appendix III
The Holy Spirit gives Spiritual Understanding

A. "Spiritual" means "Spirit-given" which means understanding given by the Holy Spirit

> *The man **without the Spirit** does not accept*
>   *the **things that come from the Spirit of God**,*
> *for they are foolishness to him, and he cannot understand them,*
>   *because **they are spiritually discerned**.*   (1 Corinthians 2:14)

1. The knowledge of divine things to which Christians are called is more than a formal acquaintance with biblical words and Christian ideas.
   a. It is to realize the reality and relevance of those activities of God the Father, Son, and Holy Spirit to which Scripture testifies.

2. Only the Holy Spirit, searcher of the deep things of God (1 Cor. 2:10), can bring about this realization in our sin-darkened minds and hearts.
   a. That is why it is called "spiritual understanding"
                                    (Col 1:9; Luke 24:25; 1 John 5:20)

3. It is not a giving of new revelation, but a work within us that enables us to grasp and to love the revelation that is there before us in the biblical text as heard and read, and as explained by teachers and writers.
   a. Sin clouds our minds and our wills so that we miss and resist the force of Scripture

B. Without the work of the Holy Spirit, God seems remote to us and unreal, and we are dull and apathetic in the face of God's truth.

1. The Spirit of God, however, opens and unveils our minds and attunes our hearts so that we can understand.
                    (see Eph. 1:17-18; 3:18-19; 2 Cor. 3:14-16; 4:6)

2. As by inspiration God provided Scripture truth for us, so now by illumination He interprets it to us.

3. Illumination is thus the applying of God's revealed truth to our hearts, so that we grasp as reality for ourselves what the sacred text sets forth.

Chapter 5, Appendix IV
The Work of God the Holy Spirit [1]

A. In the beginning the Holy Spirit is -

1. active and present at creation, hovering over the unordered conditions
   (Gen. 1:2)

B. In the Old Testament the Holy Spirit is -

1. the origin of supernatural abilities   (Gen. 41:38)
2. the giver of artistic skill   (Ex. 31:2-5)
3. the source of power and strength   (Judg. 3:9,10)
4. the inspiration of prophecy   (1 Sam. 19:20, 23)
5. the mediation of God's message   (Mic. 3:8)

C. In Old Testament prophecy the Holy Spirit is -

1. the cleansing of the heart for holy living   (Ezek. 36:25-29)

D. In salvation assurance the Holy Spirit -

1. brings conviction   (John 16:8-11)
2. regenerates the believer   (Titus 3.5)
3. sanctifies the believer   (2 Thess. 2.13)
4. completely indwells the believer   (John 14:17; Rom. 8:9-11)

E. The Holy Spirit -

1. inspired the writing of Scripture   (2 Tim. 3:16; 2 Pet. 1:21)
2. makes known spiritual truth   (John 14:26:16:13; 1 Cor. 2:13-15)
3. glorifies Christ   (John 16:14)
4. gives us power to proclaim the gospel   (Acts 1:8)
5. fills believers   (Acts 2:4)
6. pours out God's love in our heart   (Rom. 5:5)
7. enables believers to walk in holiness   (Rom. 8:1-8; Gal. 5:16-25)
8. makes intercession for us   (Rom. 8:26)
9. gives us gifts for ministry   (1 Cor. 12:4-11)
10. strengthens our inner being   (Eph. 3:16)

> The New Testament declares the Holy Spirit to be
> the assurance of the risen Lord Jesus indwelling believers.

References:

[1] The New King James Version, Spirit Filled Life Bible, Chart in the book of Acts.

CHAPTER SIX
THE NINE GIFTS OF THE HOLY SPIRIT

The nine gifts of the Holy Spirit as evidenced in 1 Corinthians 12,
are active today and did not pass away after the first century.

> *[1] Now concerning spiritual gifts, brethren, I do not want you to be ignorant:*
> *[4] There are diversities of gifts, but the same Spirit.*
> *[5] There are differences of ministries, but the same Lord.*
> *[6] And there are diversities of activities, but it is the same God who works all in all.*
> *[7] But the manifestation of the Spirit is given to each one for the profit of all:*
> *[8] for to one is given the word of wisdom through the Spirit,*
> *   to another the word of knowledge through the same Spirit,*
> *[9] to another faith by the same Spirit, to another*
> *   gifts of healings by the same Spirit,*
> *[10] to another the working of miracles, to another prophecy,*
> *   to another discerning of spirits, to another different kinds of tongues,*
> *   to another the interpretation of tongues.*
> *[11] But one and the same Spirit works all these things,*
> *   distributing to each one individually as He wills.*
>
> (1 Cor. 12: 1, 4-11)

A. WE CAN MISUNDERSTAND THE GIFTS OF THE HOLY SPIRIT

> *Now concerning spiritual gifts, brethren, I do not want you to be ignorant:*
> (1 Cor. 12: 1)

1. This verse means that we can be *"ignorant"* about spiritual gifts.
    "Ignorant" does not mean "stupid", but it means <u>not educated</u> in a subject.

2. The Corinthians misunderstood the manner in which the Holy Spirit works through individuals.
    a. They abused the use of spiritual gifts, apparently regarding the gifts as being ends in themselves.
    b. They also misunderstood the power of the Holy Spirit.

3. Paul responded by showing them:

   a. the need for varied and multiple manifestations of the Holy Spirit
                                                           (1 Cor. chapter 12)
      (manifestation means readily seen by the understanding or by the eye)
   b. the need for <u>loving</u> and <u>unselfish motives</u> in these manifestations of the Holy Spirit
                                                   (1 Cor. chapter 13)
   c. the need for <u>self-control</u> and for keeping <u>an orderly, edifying manner</u> in corporate services   (1 Cor. chapter 14)
     • <u>not</u> out of order and <u>not</u> tearing people down

4. Paul introduced three guiding principles that distinguish the ways of the Holy Spirit:

   a. The principle of conscious control-
     • They thought that the gift-operations of the Holy Spirit were a compulsive possession that overcame them or took away their own will.
     • Unlike paganism, the power of the Holy Spirit does <u>not</u> drive people into wild compulsive acts.
     • The gentle dovelike ministry of the Holy Spirit strengthens human personality.
     • The Holy Spirit empowers - He does <u>not</u> overpower.
   b. The principle that Christ is glorified-
     • All manifestations of the Holy Spirit will harmonize with the truth about Jesus.
   c. The principle of foundation faith-
     • The main work of the Holy Spirit is to bring people under the lordship of Jesus Christ.

B. DIVERSITIES (VARIOUS KINDS) OF THE GIFTS OF THE HOLY SPIRIT

> *There are diversities of gifts, but the same Spirit.*
> *There are differences of ministries, but the same Lord.*
> *And there are diversities of activities, but it is the same God who works all in all.*
>   (1 Cor. 12: 4-6)

1. The word gift means a present without any payment in return.
2. The Holy Spirit is <u>not</u> an impersonal power, and His gifts do <u>not</u> spring from a human source;
   a. His gifts are the work of God and are from the Holy Spirit - the One Whom Jesus sent -
   b. His ministries are modeled after the main minister - Jesus Christ the Son
   c. and the works of the Holy Spirit come from the chief worker - God the Father

3. Though all the gifts or abilities flow from the one God, Lord, and Spirit, the manifestation of the Holy Spirit is expressed in different ways in different individuals.
   a. The purpose of our different gifts is not to benefit ourselves alone, but to help the entire church.

b. The expression "all in all" in verse 12:6 means "<u>all</u> the gifts in <u>all</u> the persons who possess them."

C. THE MANIFESTATION OF THE HOLY SPIRIT

> *But the manifestation of the Spirit is given to each one for the profit of all:*
> (1 Cor. 12: 7)

1. The body of Christ grows to maturity in faith and love "as each part does its work" and fulfills its grace-given form of service.   (Eph. 4:16; Eph. 4:7, 12)

2. Paul identifies a spiritual gift as a supernatural ability bestowed on an individual by the Holy Spirit - <u>not</u> as a heightened natural ability

3. So, each gift is a manifestation of the Holy Spirit - that is, visible evidence of His activity.

D. GIFTS OF REVELATION – God reveals these gifts to us

> - *for to one is given the word of wisdom through the Spirit*
> - *to another the word of knowledge through the same Spirit*
> - *to another discerning of spirits*   (1 Cor 12: 8, 10c)

1. The **word of wisdom** is a spiritual message at a given moment through the Holy Spirit, that supernaturally discloses the mind, purpose, and way of God as applied to a specific situation.   (1 Kings 3:24-26; Matt. 22:15-22)

   a. When you are ministering to someone, and the Lord gives you a Word of Wisdom for that person, you will get a revelation concerning their future life and/or ministry, indicating both the current path they are on, and what God is planning for them. [6]
   b. This wisdom concerns new revelations of God's purposes, rather than human wisdom or human philosophy.   (Eph. 1:7-8; 3:10; Col. 2:2-3)

   > *For it seemed good to the Holy Spirit, and to us, to lay upon you no greater burden than these necessary things:*
   > *that you abstain from things offered to idols, from blood, from things strangled, and from sexual immorality....*   (Acts 15:28-29)

   c. A word of wisdom does <u>not have to be vocal</u>. Many times it is <u>an internal understanding</u> that has been <u>planted within by the Holy Spirit</u>. [7]

2. The **word of knowledge** is the Holy Spirit revelation of information pertaining to a person or an event, given for a specific purpose, usually having to do with an immediate need.   (Matt. 2:22; Acts 9:11-17; 10:17-23)

a. The Word of Knowledge is a supernatural impartation to you of facts concerning the person's past and present. It might be about something that happened in the person's life, or it might be a current circumstance or condition. It could even include a person's thoughts and aspirations. It could include the condition of the spirit or the body. It might include something the person doesn't even know themselves. [6]

b. The word of knowledge is the revealing of a fact in existence that can only be supernaturally revealed. It cannot be seen or heard or known naturally.

c. Look at the example of Jesus' knowledge of the marital status of the woman at the well after He told her to go get her husband:

The woman answered and said, "I have no husband."
Jesus said to her, "You have well said, 'I have no husband,' for you have had five husbands, and the one whom you now have is not your husband; in that you spoke truly."
The woman said to Him, "Sir, I perceive that You are a prophet."
(John 4:17-19)

After the woman shared the things Jesus told her with the people of her city:

*And **many** of the Samaritans of that city **believed in Him because of the word of the woman who testified**, "He told me all that I ever did."*
(John 4:39)

3. The **discerning of spirits** is the ability to comprehend the source of a spiritual manifestation- whether it is the Holy Spirit, an evil spirit, or merely the human spirit. [7]   (Acts 5:3; 8:13-24)

a. "Manifestation" means an indication of the presence of or the nature of some person.

b. It is **not mind reading**. It has nothing to do with the realm of the mind. The discerning of spirits is the **divine ability** to see **the presence and activity of a spirit** that motivates a human being, whether good or bad. [8]
Paul's interaction with Elymas is a good example:

But Elymas the sorcerer (for so his name is translated) withstood them, seeking to turn the proconsul away from the faith. Then Saul, who also is called Paul, filled with the Holy Spirit, looked intently at him and said, "O full of all deceit and all fraud, you son of the devil, you enemy of all righteousness, will you not cease perverting the straight ways of the Lord?"
(Acts 13:8-10)

c. When we are presented with something that is deceptive or runs contrary to biblical truth, the Holy Spirit will give us a "check in our spirit".

d. The Apostle John confirms that deceptive spirits will manifest in the church:

Beloved, do not believe every spirit, but test the spirits, whether they are of God; because many false prophets have gone out into the world.
(1 John 4:1)

e. Towards the end of the age, when false teachers and distortion of Biblical Christianity will greatly increase, this gift will be extremely important to the church. [9]

> *Now **the Spirit expressly says that in latter times** some will depart from the faith, **giving heed to** deceiving spirits and doctrines of demons, speaking lies in hypocrisy, having their own conscience seared with a hot iron...*
>
> (1 Timothy 4:1-2)

E. GIFTS OF POWER

> - *to another faith by the same Spirit*
> - *to another gifts of healings by the same Spirit*
> - *to another the working of miracles*   (1 Cor 12: 9, 10a)

1. The **gift of faith** is a unique form of faith that goes beyond natural faith and saving faith. It supernaturally trusts and does not doubt with reference to the specific matters involved.

   a. This gift of faith is given instantly - not like the faith that we grow in
      (Peter walk on water)   (Matt. 14:29; Acts 3:1-16)
   b. This is faith that God will use them to perform any required miracle
                                                      (Mark 11:23; James 5:13-18)
   c. Like the faith which leads to salvation, this faith relies on God and on His supernatural power   (Eph. 1:19, 20)
   d. It is God, to Whom the faith is directed, Who performs the miracle or saves- not the faith itself.

2. **Gifts of healings** are those healings performed supernaturally through the Holy Spirit.
   a. James exhorts us to call on gifts of healing pray for the sick and infirm. We must pray expectantly and with faith, but we must not pray presumptuously (take for granted; unjustified boldness; superiority) and arrogantly. God can use us to perform miraculous healings, but this will only happen <u>according to His will and timing, not ours</u>. [10]
   b. The Bible refers to "gifts of healing" in plural form – not THE gift of healing. This suggests, that healing is:
      - a transient or occasional gift. In other words (and with full apologies to "faith healers"), healing is a gift that can be exercised by any person, according to the will of the Holy Spirit. [10]
      - and that because there are many sicknesses and diseases, the gifts are related to healings of many disorders.
   c. A healing may be gradual or instantaneous and is not always 100% successful with every person. Even Paul, who healed many, was unable to heal Epaphroditis (Philippians 2:25-30). Paul said, *"...he was sick almost unto death; but God had mercy on him."* Only Jesus was able to heal <u>every time</u>.[10]

3. The **working of miracles** is a manifestation of power beyond the ordinary course of natural law. (something that has no other explanation)
   a. It is a divine enablement from God to do something that could not be done naturally.

b. Since "healings" are miracles, those miracles meant here must refer to miracles of special and extraordinary power.

c. These miracles are always <u>the power of God alone- not of any man</u>.

F. GIFTS OF SPEAKING

> - *to another prophecy*
> - *to another different kinds of tongues*
> - *to another the interpretation of tongues*   (1 Cor 12: 10b, d, e)

1. The **gift of prophecy** is a divine disclosure on behalf of the Holy Spirit, an edifying revelation of the Holy Spirit for the moment

   a. a sudden insight of the Holy Spirit, prompting exhortation or comfort
                                                              (1 Cor. 14:3, 30)

   b. a spontaneously revealed message spoken to the church or to an individual
                                                              (1 Cor. 14:1-5; 1 Tim. 4:14)

   c. Prophesy was also exercised for future events in the New Testament.
                                                              (Acts 11:27-30; 21:10-14)
   (Agabus prophecy of famine and of likely harm or death to Paul)

   d. Like the other miracles, the gift of prophecy depends on faith in God.
                                                              (Rom. 12:6)

   > *But he who prophesies speaks edification and exhortation and comfort to men. For you can all prophesy one by one, that all may learn and all may be encouraged.*   (1 Cor. 14:3, 31)

   e. edification means to instruct or benefit spiritually or morally; to be uplifted.

   f. exhortation means encouragment or gentle warning to strengthen and establish the believer in the faith. It challenges God's people to obey the truth of God's Word and warns them of the consequences of not doing so.

2. **Different kinds of tongues** is the gift of speaking supernaturally in a language not known to the individual.   (1 Cor. 13:1; Acts 2:11)

   a. Tongues are used especially for praying and singing in the Spirit and for thanksgiving and worship   (1 Cor. 14:14-19)

   b. This gift is used to personally build up the believer (1 Cor. 14:4; Jude 1:20)

   c. It is also to help us in prayer   (1 Cor. 14:15; Rom. 8:26)

3. The **interpretation of tongues** is the gift of rendering the message of the Spirit so that the message may be understood by others when exercised in public.

   a. Speaking in tongues with interpretation may at times contain a revelation, knowledge, prophecy, or teaching for the assembly of believers.[9] Paul wrote to the Corinthian church:

   > *... speaking with tongues, what shall I profit you unless I speak to you either by revelation, by knowledge, by prophesying, or by teaching? Therefore let him who speaks in a tongue pray that he may interpret.*
   >   (1 Corinthians 14:6,13)

    b. It is different from the translation of a foreign language. (This occurrence may have been the Holy Spirit causing the individuals to understand the words being spoken)

    c. The interpretation of tongues is not an operation of the human mind. It is a functioning of the Holy Spirit through the mind.

    d. The interpreter does not understand the language or the tongue that he is interpreting. The interpretation of tongues can come in two ways: The interpreter speaks the words inspirationally, or he sees what he is speaking about in the form of a vision. Paul points out that the utterance in tongues is always spoken to God, while prophecy is always spoken to man. [8]

G. THE HOLY SPIRIT DISTRIBUTES THE GIFTS

> *But one and the same Spirit works all these things,*
> *distributing to each one individually as He wills.*   (1 Cor 12: 11)

1. The Holy Spirit bestows the gifts to Whom He wills as each occasion requires.
   But the manifestation of the Spirit is given to each one for the profit of all:
   (1 Corinthians 12:7)

2. Each believer is given gifts by God to enable them to minister for Him.
   As each one has received a gift, minister it to one another, as good stewards
   of the manifold grace of God.   (1 Peter 4:10)

H. ARE THE GIFTS FOR TODAY OR DID THEY PASS AWAY WITH THE APOSTLES?

1. The promise of the gift of the Holy Spirit, His power and gifts are for *"you and your children and to all who are afar off, as many as the Lord our God shall call"*
   (Acts 2:39)

2. Paul said, *"the gifts and callings of God are without repentance* (without changing one's mind)*"*   (Rom. 11:29)

3. Paul also said, that the only time that tongues and prophesy would pass away would be when, *"that which is perfect had come"*.

    a. In the context this describes when we would see God *"face to face" and know even as we are known"*   (1 Cor. 13:8-12).

    b. This is believed to be an obvious reference to the kingdom coming to earth and when the King will be face to face with each of us. Then we will have no need of the gifts!

4. One of the many scriptures that support the operation today of the Holy Spirit in signs and wonders is Hebrews 13:8, which says,
   "Jesus Christ is the same, yesterday, today, and forever."

5. As Jesus and the Father are eternally the same, they will act the same and deal in the same manner with their children.
   a. God always treats His children with grace.
   b. The Greek word for grace is "*charis*", which is also translated "*gift.*"
   c. If God's grace has not disappeared, how then can the gifts of His grace disappear?

6. In the Bible we are told to pray and expect miracles, but the performing of these signs is totally up to God (James 5:14).
   a. This is not a promise limited to a time or culture.
   b. It is a scriptural universal command with a promise that goes with it.
   c. We are responsible only to pray and wait on God Who is responsible for the results.

7. Historically there is proof that the gifts continued throughout church history.
   a. Irenaeus (140-203 A.D.) was a prominent church leader who strived to clarify which writings were true canon of scripture, and he had seen tongues, the gift of prophesy and the word of knowledge in his day. http://www.britannica.com/EBchecked/topic/293911/Saint-Irenaeus
   b. Justin Martyr (155 A.D.) saw men and women possess gifts of the spirit. He was an early Christian apologist who worked to present the rational basis for the Christian faith, to defend the faith against objections, and he exposed the flaws of other world views, and is regarded as the foremost interpreter in the 2nd century of the theory of the Word of God.
   c. Tertullian (220 A.D.) saw healings and wrote on the whole reorganization of human life on a Christian basis
   d. Augustine (354-430 A.D.) spoke of tongues and saw healings.
   e. During the revivals throughout the 1700's, the church expected the Holy Spirit to manifest His presence in powerful, visible ways.
   f. In the early 1800's, the early Quakers and Methodists experienced the gifts of the Spirit.

References:

[1] Packer, J.I., *Concise Theology: A Guide to Historic Christian Beliefs*, 1993
[2] Carr, Pastor Steve, *Discipleship Series*, Calvary Chapel, Arroyo Grande, CA, *http://calvaryag.org/index.php?option=com_content&view=article&id=32&Itemid=43*
[3] Hayford, Dr. Jack, *New King James Version Spirit Filled Bible*, Jack Hayford Commentary, Thomas Nelson Publishers, 1991
[4] Douglas, J. D., General Editor, Comfort, Philip W., New Testament Editor, *New Testament Volume, New Commentary on the Whole Bible*
[5] *http://wattsteachingministries.org/images/Sermon_040311_The_Baptism_with_the_Holy_Spirit_Part_9.pdf*
[6] Crause, Les D., *The Word of Wisdom*, AMI, San Diego, CA. 2012
[7] Duffield, Dr. Guy P., and Van Cleave, Nathaniel M., *Foundations of Pentecostal theology*, 1987
[8] Sumrall, Lester, *Gifts and Ministries of the Holy Spirit*, 1982
[9] Stamps, Donald C., *The Full Life Study Bible*, 1992
[10] *http://www.contenderministries.org/biblestudy/giftsofthespirit4.php*

Chapter 6, Appendix I
The Acts of the Holy Spirit [1]

A. **The Book of Acts tells what Jesus Christ the risen Lord continues to do and teach through the Holy Spirit.**
   1. Acts is a record of practicing Christianity under the power of the Holy Spirit.
   2. It teaches believers how to live, together in meaningful Christian fellowship, sharing freely with one another.   (Acts 2:42; 4:32- 35)
   3. It also shows that Christians 'inevitably will have disagreements (Acts 6: 1; 11: 1-3; 15:2, 7; 15:36-39), but that God gives wisdom and grace to settle differences (Acts 15: 12-22).
   4. Even though the early church had its share of strong personalities, there was still a willingness to listen and to submit to one another   (Acts 15:6-14)

B. **Probably the most prominent characteristic of the early Christians was the power of the Holy Spirit demonstrated through them.**
   1. They fasted and prayed fervently (Acts 2:42; 6:4; 13:3), and their faith released the miracle-working power of God (Acts 3:16).
   2. Acts is about ordinary people doing extraordinary things.
   3. Signs followed those who believed! See Mark 16: 17, 18.

   Then the resurrection of Jesus is emphasized, particularly as the fulfillment of Old Testament prophecy and as God's reversal of men's verdict on Jesus
                    (Acts 1:-3; 2:24-32; 4: 10; 5:30; 10:40,41; 13:30-37; 17:31)
   The apostles declare that Jesus has been exalted to a position of unique and universal dominion.   (Acts 2:33-36; 3:21; 5:31)

C. **From that place of supreme honor and executive power Jesus had poured out the promised Holy Spirit (2:33)**
   1. The Holy Spirit bears witness 'to Him   (Acts 5:32)
   2. and empowers believers   (Acts 1:8)
   3. Jesus has been "ordained by God to be Judge of the living and the dead" (10:42) and will return in triumph at the end of the age   (Acts 1: 11)
   4. Meanwhile, those who believe in Him will receive forgiveness of sins (2:21; 3:19; 4:12; 5:31; 10:43; 13:38, 39) and "the gift of the Holy Spirit"   (Acts 2:38)
   5. Those who do not believe in Him are destined for terrible things   (Acts 3:23)

D. **The power of the Holy Spirit through the church is the most striking feature in Acts.**
   1. The book has also been called by some "The Acts of the Holy Spirit.'
   2. The work of the Spirit in Acts, however, cannot be understood without seeing the relationship between Acts and the Gospels, which demonstrates an essential continuity.
   3. Both the public ministry of Jesus in the Gospels and the public ministry of the church in Acts begin with a life-changing- encounter with the Spirit; both are essential accounts of the results of that event.

E. **The power of the Holy Spirit in Jesus' life authorized Him to preach the kingdom of God and to demonstrate kingdom power by healing the sick, casting out demons, and setting the captives free.**   (Luke 4:14-19; Matt. 4:23)
   1. The Book of Acts is the story of the disciples receiving what Jesus received in order to do what Jesus did.

F. Luke's terminology the Book of Acts in describing people's experience with the Holy Spirit in Acts is fluid.

He notes that people were:
1. "filled with the Holy Spirit"   (Acts 2:4; 9: 17)
2. that "they received the Holy Spirit"   (Acts 8: 17)
3. that "the Holy Spirit fell upon [them]"   (Acts 10:44)
4. that "the Holy Spirit had been poured out on [them]"   (Acts 10:45)
5. and that "the Holy Spirit came upon them"   (Acts 19:6)

These are all then essential equivalents of Jesus' promise that the church would "be baptized with the Holy Spirit" (Acts 1:5; see especially its immediate fulfillment in Acts 2:4, which Luke describes as a filling).

G. Three of these five instances record specific special manifestations of the Spirit in which the people themselves participated.
1. Those on the Day of Pentecost and the Gentiles of Cornelius's house spoke with other tongues   (Acts 2:4; 10:46)
2. The Ephesians "spoke with tongues and prophesied"   (Acts 19:6).
3. Although it is not specified, it is generally agreed that there was also some type of manifestation in which the Samaritans participated, because Luke says that "when Simon saw that ... the Holy Spirit was given"   (Acts 8: 18)

References:

[1] Hayford, Dr. Jack, *New King James Version Spirit Filled Bible*, Introduction to Acts, Thomas Nelson Publishers, 1991

Chapter 6, Appendix II
Healing and Deliverance by Jesus in the Gospels

1	John 4:46	The Nobleman's Son
2	Mark 1:21, Luke 4:31	The Man with an Unclean Spirit
3	Matt 8:14, Mark 1:29, Luke 4:38	Simon Peter's Mother-in-Law
4	Matt 8:1, Mark 1:40, Luke 5:12	The Healing of the Leper
5	Matt 9:1, Mark 2:1, Luke 5:17	The Healing of the Paralytic
6	John. 5:2	The Man at Bethesda pool
7	Matt 12:9, Mark 3:1, Luke 6:6	The Man with the Withered Hand
8	Matt 8:5; Luke 7:2	The Centurion's Servant
9	Luke 7:11	Widow's Deceased Son
10	Matt 8:28; Mark 5:1; Luke 8:26	Demoniacs at Gadara
11	Matt 9:20; Mark 5:25; Luke 8:43	Woman with the Issue of Blood
12	Matt 9:18; Mark 5:21; Luke 8:40	Jairus's Deceased Daughter
13	Matt 9:27	Two Blind Men
14	Matt 9:32	Mute, Possessed Man
15	Matt 15:21; Mark 4:24	Daughter of Canaanite
16	Mark 7:32	Deaf Man with Impediment
17	Mark 8:22	Blind Man at Bethsaida
18	Matt 17:14; Mark 9:14; Luke 9:37	Epileptic Boy
19	John 9:1	Man Born Blind
20	Matt 12:22; Luke 11:14	Man, Blind, Dumb, Possessed
21	Luke 13:10	Woman Bent Double
22	Luke 14:1	Man with Dropsy
23	John 11:11	Lazarus
24	Luke 17:11	Ten Lepers
25	Matt 20:29; Mark 10:45; Luke 18:35	Blind Bartimaeus
26	Luke 22:50	Healed the ear of Malchus, servant of the high priest

Chapter 6, Appendix III
Healing and Deliverance in the Book of Acts

1	Acts 3:1-8	Peter healed man lame since birth in the name of Jesus Christ of Nazareth
2	Acts 5:12	Many signs and wonders by the hands of the apostles
3	Acts 5:15-16	The people brought a multitude of sick, and those with unclean spirits, and every one was healed.
4	Acts 8:6-7	God performed miracles through Philip, and people were healed and were delivered from unclean spirits.
5	Acts 9:17-18	The Lord Jesus sent Ananias to put his hands on Saul for Saul to receive his sight and be filled with the Holy Spirit.
6	Acts 9:32-35	Aeneas in Lydda was in bed eight years, sick of the palsy. Peter said, Jesus Christ make you whole: arise and make your bed. And he arose immediately. And all that lived in Lydda and Saron saw him, and turned to the Lord.
7	Acts 9:36-42	Peter prayed for a disciple, a lady named Dorcas who had died, and raised her from the dead.
8	Acts 10:38-39a	*"… God anointed Jesus of Nazareth with the Holy Spirit and with power, who went about doing good and healing all who were oppressed by the devil, for God was with Him. And we are witnesses of all things which He did both in the land of the Jews and in Jerusalem"*
9	Acts 14:3	*"Therefore they stayed there a long time, speaking boldly in the Lord, who was bearing witness to the word of His grace, granting signs and wonders to be done by their hands."*
10	Acts 14:7-10	Paul preached the Gospel at Lystra and healed a man crippled from birth who never had walked. Paul told him to stand upright, and the man leaped and walked.

11	Acts 14:19-20	The people stoned Paul, and threw him out of the city, thinking he was dead. But the disciples stood around about him, he rose up, and went back into the city.
12	Acts 16:16-18	Paul commanded in the name of Jesus Christ that a spirit come out of a woman, and it came out of her.
13	Acts 19:11-12	God performed special miracles by the hands of Paul so that diseases and evil spirits went out of the people.
14	Acts 20:9-12	Paul raised a young man from the dead, named Eutychus who had fallen 3 stories
15	Acts 28:3-6	Paul was bitten by a poisonous snake, shook off the beast into the fire, and was not harmed.
16	Acts 28:7-9	Paul laid hands on and prayed for the father of an island ruler who was sick with a fever coughing up blood, and the man was healed. Others on the island with diseases came to Paul and were also healed.

Chapter 6, Appendix IV
God Still Heals the sick and saves the lost in the name of the Lord Jesus Christ

Marilyn Hickey Shows God's Healing Power to 400,000 in Pakistan Jan 2012

Evangelist and Bible teacher Marilyn Hickey from Colorado believes in modern-day miracles through God's healing power and shared with The Christian Post her latest prayer initiative in Karachi, Pakistan, which exposed over 400,000 people to Jesus Christ.

Karachi is the largest Muslim city in the world. – with an estimated 18 million residents. According to Time magazine's January 2012 assessment, it's also the most dangerous city in the world. But Hickey is boldly taking God's healing and love to the Muslim-dominated nation.

The 80-year-old told The Christian Post that she had been traveling to Pakistan since 1995 and has a "great heart" for the people. According to Hickey, her healing meetings draw huge audiences, with about 75 percent of them Muslim attendees. She explained that she first teaches about one miracle of Jesus – sharing his healing power.
A record number of people attended the three nights of healing meetings at the Karachi YMCA compound. By the third night, the attendance was up to 200,000. The streets leading to the compound had to be shut down as thousands were positioned outside the ground's walls watching the event on large screens.

"Then I pray for everything," Hickey said. "I have them stand and put their hand on their head and pray for everything [things plaguing their lives – diseases, etc]." Following the prayer, audience members who notice a significant difference in the state of their afflictions are urged to come forward and give testimony to the miracles they experienced. Multiple healings were reported, including a Muslim man who was paralyzed can now walk one man, who had a tumor behind his ear, reportedly had the cancer disappear following the prayer, and a little boy blind from birth can now see, and captured on video.

"So they come and testify," she stated. "And I acknowledge that it's in the name of Jesus I pray. I say, 'Jesus healed you.'"

Hickey says that the greatest miracle she witnessed was when Christ came into her life. "When I was 16, I prayed. That was the greatest miracle of my life. I invited Jesus to come in, to be a part of my life, and to forgive my sins."

"I don't go in there to convert. I can't convert anyone. I go to help [people] have encounters with Jesus. There are always going to be people who think you shouldn't do anything spiritual, but I don't think you can let [that deter you]."

References:

[1] *The Christian Post* 2/12/12 and *Charisma News* 1/31/12)

CHAPTER SEVEN
SHARE THE GOOD NEWS OF THE KINGDOM

*Every Christian is called to
share the good news of God's kingdom:
The Gospel of Jesus Christ.*

His kingdom
come,
His will be done

*And Jesus said to them,
"Go into all the world and
preach the gospel to every creature."
(Mark 16:15)*

A. "The Gospel" literally means "the good news" and is about Jesus, Whom Mark identifies by name and title. The word "gospel" appears 98 times in the New Testament.

The beginning of the gospel of Jesus Christ, the Son of God. (Mark 1:1)

Paul wrote in the book of Romans:

*Paul, **a bondservant of Jesus Christ**,
called to be an apostle,
separated to the gospel of God
which He promised before through His prophets in the Holy Scriptures,
concerning His Son Jesus Christ our Lord* (Romans 1: 1-3)

Also see the law
of the bondservant
in Ex. 21:1-6

The word *Gospel* includes:
1. the promise of salvation
2. its fulfillment by the life, death, resurrection, and ascension of Jesus Christ
3. *The Gospel* also came to mean the books of Matthew, Mark, Luke, and John

B. The Holy Spirit anointed the Lord Jesus to preach the good news.

*"The Spirit of the LORD is upon Me,
because He has anointed Me
to preach the gospel to the poor;*
*He has sent Me to heal the brokenhearted,
to proclaim liberty to the captives
and recovery of sight to the blind,
to set at liberty those who are oppressed;"* (Luke 4: 18)

Prophesied by
Isaiah 700 years
before Jesus
(Isaiah 61:1)

1. In Matthew 4: 12 and 23, the Bible says that when the Lord Jesus began His earthly ministry, He began to preach;
   *"Repent, for **the kingdom of heaven** has come near"*
   "Jesus went throughout Galillee, teaching in their synagogues,
   *proclaiming **the good news of the kingdom**,*
   and healing every disease and sickness among the people."

   > The kingdom is so important to God that He mentions it
   > more than 100 times in the New Testament.

2. In Matthew 6, Jesus told Hs disciples that they should pray this way:
   "Our Father in heaven, hallowed be Your name, Your kingdom come,
   Your will be done, on earth as it is in heaven ..."

C. We are called to share our faith with those who don't know Christ.

Jesus said:
"For the Son of Man has come to seek and to save that which was lost."
(Luke 19:10)

Jesus is the shepherd who will leave *"the ninety-nine sheep in the wilderness, and go after the one which is lost until he finds it"* (Luke 15:4)

> Jesus carries the lost sheep on His shoulders and rejoices that it is found

D. God wants to make us an effective witness for Him as He enlists us as a co-laborer in His great work of redemption.

For we are God's fellow workers;
you are God's field, you are God's building. (1 Cor. 3:9)

*Now, therefore, you are **no longer strangers and foreigners**, but fellow citizens with the saints and members of the household of God, having been built on the foundation of the apostles and prophets, Jesus Christ Himself being the chief cornerstone, in whom the whole building, being fitted together, grows into a holy temple in **the Lord, in whom you also are being built together for a dwelling place of God in the Spirit**.* (Eph. 2: 19-22)

God wants to give us the same love and concern **that Jesus Himself has** for those He longs to redeem.

E. We have been called to the ministry of reconciliation (to bring others as friends to Jesus).

> *Now all things are of God, **who has reconciled us to Himself through Jesus Christ,***
>> ***and has given us the ministry of reconciliation**, that is,*
>> *that God was in Christ **reconciling** the world to Himself,*
>> *not imputing their trespasses to them,*
>> *and has committed to us the **word of reconciliation.***
> *Now then, we are **ambassadors for Christ,***
>> *as though **God were pleading through us***:
> *We <u>implore you</u> on Christ's behalf, **<u>be reconciled to God</u>**.*   (2 Cor. 5:18-20)

Every believer <u>has been called</u> to <u>Jesus' ministry</u> of reconciling others back to God.
<u>reconcile</u> – Jesus removed the separation of the curtain from top to bottom
<u>plead</u> – God's emotional or earnest appeal
<u>implore</u>– God cries out/pleads through us

F. We are called to be a light to this world.
Jesus charged His disciples from the very beginning by telling them to shine His light into the darkness.

> *"**You are the light of the world.***
> *A city that is set on a hill cannot be hidden.*
> *Nor do they light a lamp and put it under a basket, but on a lampstand,*
> *and it gives light to all who are in the house.*
> *Let your light so shine before men, that they may see your good works and*
> *glorify your Father in heaven. "*   (Matt. 5:14-16)

> (say "I am the light of the world")
> (say "It is <u>not</u> secret faith")

By sharing our faith with others we are letting His light shine through us.

G. We are to publicly and openly proclaim His praises.
In his first letter to the persecuted Christians, Peter encouraged every follower of Christ to understand their very important position as His own special people.

> *But you are a chosen generation, a royal priesthood, a holy nation,*
> ***His own special people**, that you may proclaim the praises of Him*
> *Who called you out of darkness into His marvelous light.*   1 Peter 2:9)

As we learn to share our faith, our message should always incorporate our personal testimony about **how He called us out of darkness**.

H. We are to teach (disciple) and to share the good news of Jesus everywhere we go.

> *And Jesus came and spoke to them, saying,*
> *"All authority has been given to Me in heaven and on earth.*
> *Go therefore and make disciples of all the nations ... "*   (Matt. 28:18-19)

Remember that we are a Christian today because someone shared Christ with us.

I. Jesus promised to teach us how to spread the Gospel.
1. Jesus didn't simply command the disciples to go preach and not fully equip them to fulfill His command.

2. By God's grace, He will make us an able and effective witness for Him:

3. If we will simply allow Jesus, He will to teach us the way He (Jesus) promised:

> *"Follow Me, and I will <u>make you become fishers of men.</u>"*   (Mark 1:17)

This promise implies several things:
1. If Jesus has to make us to become fishers of men, then we are not one naturally. Jesus spent three years and much effort training His disciples to be fishers of men.   (Matt. 10:5-42; Luke 10:1-24)

2. If He begins this work of making us a fisher of men, He will complete it.   (Phil. 1:6)

3. It is God that is at work to make us an effective witness for Him.

4. We must follow Jesus Christ fully **in all aspects of our personal life** for this work to be accomplished in us.

J. Jesus' Instructions on How to Witness for Him

> *But you shall receive power when the Holy Spirit has come upon you;*
> *and you shall be witnesses to Me in Jerusalem,*
> *and in all Judea and Samaria, and to the end of the earth."*   (Acts 1: 8)

K. Jesus encouraged us to pray for God to send workers for the Gospel.

When the disciples of Christ first began to understand the great need of the salvation of the world and the great harvest the souls as Jesus described it, Christ told them to do one essential thing - **PRAY**.   Jesus said:

> *"The harvest truly is plentiful, but the laborers are few.*
> *Therefore **pray the Lord of the harvest to send out laborers into His harvest**."*
>   (Matt. 9:37-38)

Why would Jesus encourage them to pray?
1. Because prayer will be how we will come into agreement with the Father and receive the same burden that He possesses for the lost.

2. As we begin praying for the Father to send laborers into the harvest the most natural thing that will occur will be that we will end by praying - ***"Send me Lord"***.

L. The Gospel Message in America

The Gospel message is **not getting out** in America as it should.
Look at the results of two polls taken on Easter 2012 and Easter 2013.

1. The percent of Americans **that believe** in the Resurrection of Jesus Christ **dropped** from 77% in 2012 to 64% in 2013.

2. The difference between the two polls shows a 13 point **drop in the number of Americans who believe** that Jesus Christ rose from the dead.

3. We must get past the ideas that preaching the gospel is the job only of pastors and missionaries. God is calling us to be conformed to the image of His Son – Whose heart is seek the lost.

> *My house is full, but my field is empty,*
> *who will go and work for me today?*
> *It seems my children all want to stay around my table*
> *But no one wants to work in my field,*
> *no one wants to work in my field.*
>
> *"My House is Full", song by Lanny Wolfe 1977*

M. "He who believes in Me … out of his heart will flow rivers of living water."

> *Jesus said to him,*
> *"You shall love the LORD your God with all your heart, with all your soul,*
> *and with all your mind."*   (Matt. 22: 37)

1. If we do not make this **the supreme priority of our life** because we do not come to Him on a regular basis, then His river of life within us will slowly run dry.

> *On the last day, that great day of the feast, Jesus stood and cried out, saying,*
> ***"If anyone thirsts, let him come to Me and drink.***
> ***He who believes in Me, as the Scripture has said,***
> ***out of his heart will flow rivers of living water."***
> *But this He spoke concerning the Spirit,*
> *whom those believing in Him would receive;*
> *for the Holy Spirit was not yet given,*
> *because Jesus was not yet glorified.*   (John 7:37-39)

References:

[1] *Capstone Connections,* New Members Class, *www.thecapstone.org*
[2] Carr, Pastor Steve, *Discipleship Series,* Calvary Chapel, Arroyo Grande, CA,
http://calvaryag.org/index.php?option=com_content&view=article&id=32&Itemid=43

Chapter 7, Appendix I
Capstone Church's Mission – "Tell Somebody"

A. Our love for God and for our fellow man

1. Matthew 22:37-38 is often called **the Great Commandment**.
2. Verse 39 of that same chapter is said to be "like" the Great Commandment.
3. That means that it is of the same motivation, cut from the same cloth.

> ^{37} *Jesus said to him,*
> *"'You shall love the Lord your God with all your heart, with all your soul, and with all your mind.'*
> ^{38} *This is the first and great commandment.*
> ^{39} *And the second is like it: "You shall love your neighbor as yourself."*
>
> (Matthew 22:39)

4. We know at Capstone that we cannot separate love for God and love for our fellow man.
5. And God has given us this command:

> *And this commandment we have from Him:*
> *that he who loves God must love his brother also.*   (1 John 4:21)

> Jesus said:
> *"You have heard that it was said,*
> *'You shall love your neighbor and hate your enemy.'*
> *But I say to you, love your enemies, bless those who curse you,*
> *do good to those who hate you, and pray for those who spitefully use you*
> *and persecute you that you may be sons of your Father in heaven;*
> *for He makes His sun rise on the evil and on the good,*
> *and sends rain on the just and on the unjust."*   (Matthew 5:43-45)

B. Our mission at Capstone is to *Tell Somebody*.

1. Intricately entwined within our love for God is our command to love "somebody".
2. Love is active; which means we are actively involved in vocal and practical expressions of love for "somebody" at all times.
3. At Capstone, you will always be prompted to share the love of God with "somebody".
4. It is called the Great Commission, and it is our life blood and our destiny.

5. Who are the "somebodies" God has placed in your life... at work, home, and your neighborhood? Tell them about Jesus, about eternal life, and about His church.

> *And He (Jesus) said to them,*
> *"Go into all the world and preach the gospel to every creature."*
> (Mark 16:15)
>
> ***And daily in the temple, and in every house,***
> ***they did not cease teaching and preaching Jesus as the Christ.***
> (Acts 5:42)

C. Relationship, fellowship, and instruction within the Body of Christ

1. The second great commandment is that we must love and have a real relationship with believers within the church.

2. Every believer must be connected to the Body of Christ like every member of our physical body is connected to another part of our physical body.

> *For as we have many members in one body,*
> *but all the members do not have the same function,*
> *so we, being many, are one body in Christ,*
> *and individually members of one another.*   (Rom. 12:4-5)

3. Seek the life-blood of fellowship within the Body and seek encouragement from God's Word.

4. If we stay connected to the head- Jesus Christ - we will not dry up like a branch cut off from the vine.

CHAPTER EIGHT
JESUS CHRIST IS COMING AGAIN

Jesus Christ will return at any time
and will come to rule as King
upon the earth with the saints.

Jesus declared,
"When the Son of Man comes in his glory,
and all the angels with him,
He will sit on his throne in heavenly glory"
(Matthew 25:31)

A. The importance of the Second Coming of Jesus Christ

1. It was the theme of 6 different Old Testament prophets
   (Is. 24:1-23; Is. 35:1-10; *Jer. 30,31; Dan. 2,7,12; Joel 3:1-21;*
   Zech. 14:1-12; Mal. 4:1-6)
2. Jesus Himself constantly bore witness to His Return
   (John 14:3; Matt. 24,25; Mark 13; John 21:22)
3. Paul wrote two entire letters to churches concerning the fact of the Second
   Coming of Jesus Christ   *(1 Thess. & 2 Thess.)*
4. The other apostles believed the same thing
   (Acts 3:19-21; 1 John 2:28; Jude 14-15)
5. Even the angels testified when Jesus ascended into heaven that Jesus will come
   again.   *(Acts 1:11)*

B. The purpose of these promises in Scripture about the Return of Jesus Christ

1. to encourage us to look for His Coming   *(Titus 2:13 ; 2 Pet. 3:12,13)*
2. to encourage us with hope   *(Titus 2:11-13)*
3. to encourage holy living and godliness   *(2 Pet. 3:11,14)*
4. to encourage us to be ready   *(Matt. 24:44)*
5. to encourage us to pray that we might be accounted worthy to escape His
   judgment   *(Luke 21:36)*
6. and to comfort our hearts   *(1 Thess. 4:18)*

C. The Manner of His Second Coming   (How will Jesus come back?)

1. Jesus will personally, visibly and in bodily form return so that every eye will see
   Him   *(Acts 1:11; 1 Thess. 4:16-17; Rev. 1:7; Matt. 24:30)*
2. The heavens will roll back like a scroll to reveal His Coming
   (Rev. 6:14-17; Is. 34:4)

3. His return will be sudden and without warning to those who are not looking for Him *(Matt. 24:27; Matt. 24:31-51)*
4. His return will be with power and great glory *(Matt. 24:30)*

D. The Purpose of His Second Coming   (Why is Jesus coming back?)

1. to fulfill His Word to us   *(Matt. 24:34,35) (John 14:3)*
2. to fulfill His promises to the Jews concerning the Kingdom Age
   (Is. 35:1-10; 2:1-5)
3. to fulfill His Word to judge the World   *(Matt. 25:32-46)*
4. to glorify all believers   *(Col. 3:3,4)*
5. to reward all believers   *(Matt. 16:27)*

E. The 4 Signs That We Should Look for

1. **Israel being restored as a nation**.
   This sign is directly related to His Second Coming and the end of the world. ***Israel became a nation again in 1948***.   *(Joel 3:1-21; Ezek. 37; Ps. 102:16; Ps. 14:7; Micah 4:6,7; Zeph. 3:14-20; Rom. 11:12,15, 25-27)*

2. **The formation of a ten nation organization in Europe.**   (Dan. 2:1-44)
   (covering the same general area of the ancient Roman Empire)

   God revealed to Daniel in the interpretation of a dream that the king of Babylon had one night upon his bed. The interpretation revealed that each part of the image were the kingdoms of man, and the Kingdom of God that will consume these kingdoms and will stand forever   *(Dan. 2:36-45)*. Notice verse 44, *"…in the days of these kings the God of heaven will set up a Kingdom which shall never be destroyed."*

   For a similar vision of Daniel more detailed study on this subject see *Dan. 7:1-28.*

   - *The European Community is a possible fulfillment of this prophecy.*
   - *It is amazing that the Euro currency replaced so many of Europe's currencies, including the elimination of the 3,000 year old Greek Drachma.*

3. **Nations coming together against Israel.**
   Ezekiel prophesied more than 2,500 years ago about the nations that would later come together to fight the great war with Israel.

   Now, today we are seeing the nations that Ezekiel described coming together under radical Islam and Russia with a hatred of the nation of Israel.

   Ezekiel said after the regathering of the Jews back into their land, that there will be a great war between Israel and a group of nations that will come from the far north   *(Ezek. 38:1-6; 39:1,2; See the context of Ezekiel 36, 37, 38 and 39).*

The principle nations he prophesied in this attack are Gog of the land of Magog, Meshech and Tubal. This area **today** would cover the modern States of <u>southern Russia, Georgia, Armenia, Azerbaijan, Kazakistan, Turkmenistan, Uzbekistan, Kyrgyzstan and Tajikistan</u>.

Meshech, according to the Greek historian Herodotus, settled in the mountains south-east of the Black Sea, and to the north of the ancient Assyrian empire. This area **today** would cover the modern States of <u>Georgia, Armenia, Azerbiajan, parts of Turkey, Syria and Iraq</u>.
(same as in Ezekiel except added parts of Turkey, Syria, and Iraq)

See map below.

There will be many other nations that come together for this war with Israel.
Yet, the Bible is clear, they are all destroyed.

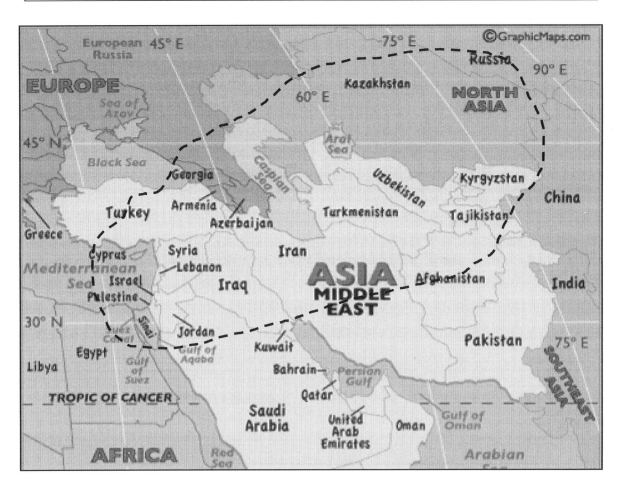

4. **These days "will be like the days of Noah"**   (Matt. 24:37-39)

What were the days of Noah like?
a. The earth was corrupt before God   *(Gen. 6:11)*
b. The earth was filled with violence   *(Gen. 6:11)*
c. The people's imagination was only continually evil   *(Gen. 6:5)*
d. The wickedness of man was great   *(Gen. 6:5; Matt. 24:12)*

> *See Chapter 8 Appendix III:*
> *Days of Noah - Prayer of Repentance for our Nation*

F. What Happens Just Prior to the Second Coming of Jesus?

1. The rapture of the Church (Also see Appendix II in this lesson chapter)
   a. What is the Rapture?
      This is when Jesus comes and takes the Church from the earth.

      > *For the Lord Himself will descend from heaven with a shout, with the voice of an archangel, and with the trumpet of God. And the dead in Christ will rise first. Then we who are alive and remain shall be caught up together with them in the clouds to meet the Lord in the air. And thus we shall always be with the Lord.*   (1 Thess. 4:16-17)

   b. The Greek word for caught up means to seize, carry off or snatch away. The word **rapture** comes from the Latin version of this text.
      Also see: *(Luke 17:26-36; 1 Cor. 15:51-54).*

   c. When will the rapture happen?
      1) There is no way to be absolutely sure on this fact, because Jesus said, "no man knows the day or hour"   (Matt. 24:36)
      2) Some believe the Rapture will be during or after the return of Jesus. Yet the weight of Scripture leads one to believe the Rapture occurs before the Tribulation period.
      3) The Tribulation period is the wrath of God coming upon the earth
                                                        (Rev. 6:16; 15:1)
      4) Yet God promises the saints that He has not appointed us to wrath but has delivered us from the wrath to come.   (1 Thess. 5:9; Rev. 1:10)
      5) A special promise to those who keep His commandments: He will keep them from the hour of trial which shall come on the whole world
                                                        (Rev. 3:10)
      6) Jesus told His disciples to pray always to escape the Tribulation period that He had just described to them   (Luke 21:36)
      7) The Biblical illustrations of Noah and Lot being delivered from God's wrath on unbelievers. They are used as examples to us.
                                                        (Luke 17:26-36; 2 Peter 2:9)
      8) God's example that He won't destroy the righteous with the wicked
                                                        (Gen. 18:23-33)

G. The Rapture and the Second Coming of Christ - Is There a Difference? [4]

1. According to some Bible scholars, prophetic Scriptures seem to speak of two separate events—the Rapture and the Second Coming of Christ.
   a. The Rapture will occur when Jesus Christ returns for his church. This is when all true believers in Christ will be taken from the earth by God into heaven
      (1 Corinthians 15:51-52; 1 Thessalonians 4:16-17)
   b. The Second Coming is when Jesus Christ returns with the church to defeat the antichrist, overthrow evil and then establish His thousand year reign
      (Revelation 19:11-16)

2. Meeting in the Air - versus - Returning with Him
   a. In the Rapture, believers meet the Lord in the air (1 Thessalonians 4:16-17)
   b. In the Second Coming, believers return with the Lord   (Revelation 19:14)

3. Before Tribulation - versus - After Tribulation
   a. The Rapture will happen before the Tribulation
      (1 Thessalonians 5:9; Revelation 3:10)
   b. The Second Coming will happen at the end of the Tribulation
      (Revelation 6-19)

4. Deliverance - versus - Judgment
   a. In the Rapture believers are taken from the earth by God as an act of deliverance.   (1 Thessalonians 4:13-17; 5:9)
   b. In the Second Coming unbelievers are removed from the earth by God as an act of judgment.   (Revelation 3:10; 19:11-21)

5. Hidden - versus - Seen by All
   a. The Rapture, according to Scripture, will be an instantaneous, hidden event.
      (1 Corinthians 15:50-54)
   b. The Second Coming, according to Scripture, will be seen by everyone.
      (Revelation 1:7)

6. At Any Moment - versus - Only After Certain Events
   a. The Rapture could happen at any moment.
      (1 Corinthians 15:50-54; Titus 2:13; 1 Thessalonians 4:14-18)
   b. The Second Coming won't happen until certain events take place.
      (2 Thessalonians 2:4 Matthew 24:15-30 Revelation 6-18)

H. The Tribulation Period and the Second Coming of Christ

1. The Tribulation Period- This is a separate study of the seven year period of time preceding the Second Coming of Christ and the Battle of Armageddon

2. Second Coming of Christ- This is a separate study of the Antichrist, the thousand year reign of Christ upon the earth when Satan is bound, the judgment seat of Christ, the losing of Satan and his being cast into the lake of fire, The Great White Throne Judgment, the first earth and heaven are passed away and God creates a New heaven and earth. We will live with Him throughout eternity

I. As a member of His Living Church, His Body, Jesus calls you and me:

1. To always live in faithful anticipation of Jesus' return.
(Rev 2:25; 3:11; 16:15; 22:7, 12, 20)
2. To stand firm when experiencing apparent defeat, being confident of ultimate victory   (Rev. 13:7-10; 14:9-13; 19:1-10)
3. To faithful intercessory prayer and constant praise-filled worship "Unto Him Who is worthy!"   (Rev. 5:8-10)
4. To hear the Spirit's voice, to know the Father's Word, and to walk the Savior's pathway of obedience.   (Rev. 2:7, 11, 17, 26-29; 3:5, 6, *12-18, 21, 22*)
5. To anticipate an eternal destiny of joy and purpose with Christ.
(Rev. 19:1-10; 20:4-6; 21:1-22:4)

J. Can anyone predict the time of Jesus' coming? (see chapter 8 appendix IV)

1. Jesus made it clear that some day He will come again to establish His authority over the whole world — and this should give us great hope, no matter how gloomy or frightening the headlines may be.
Jesus declared,
"When the Son of Man comes in his glory, and all the angels with him, he will sit on his throne in heavenly glory"   *(Matthew 25:31)*

2. Jesus warned us <u>not to try to predict</u> exactly when this will happen.

3. Over the centuries, many people have ignored this and claimed to know exactly when Jesus was coming — but without exception they were <u>proven wrong</u>.
Jesus said,
"No one knows about that day or hour, not even the angels in heaven, nor the Son, but only the Father"   (Mark 13:32)

4. However, Jesus did tell us that certain things must happen before He returns — and these are like signposts pointing to His coming.
    a. For example, He told us that before He comes again, the Gospel must be preached to the whole world, and only then would the present age come to an end.   *(see Mark 13:10)*
    b. And surely this is coming true today, through new technologies that can reach almost every corner of the earth with the Gospel !

5. The real issue, however, is this**:   Are each of us ready for His coming?**
    a. Even if His coming is delayed, am I ready to meet Him — as I will some day?
    b. We can make sure of our salvation by turning to Jesus Christ and by faith trusting Him as our Lord and Savior today.

God's Everlasting Love

What then shall we say to these things? If God is for us,
who can be against us?
He who did not spare His own Son, but delivered Him up for us all,
how shall He not with Him also freely give us all things?
Who shall bring a charge against God's elect? It is God who justifies.
Who is he who condemns?
It is Christ who died, and furthermore is also risen,
who is even at the right hand of God,
who also makes intercession for us.   (Romans 8: 31-34)

  ○   It is Jesus Christ Who will be the Judge over all the earth

  ○   But He does <u>not condemn us</u>, and even now He makes intercession
       for us (brings requests to God the Father for us).

Finally, there is laid up for me the crown of righteousness, which the
Lord, the righteous Judge, will give to me on that Day, and not to me
*only but also **to all who have loved His appearing.***
                                                              (2 Timothy 4:8)

References:

[1] Carr, Pastor Steve, *Discipleship Series*, Calvary Chapel, Arroyo Grande, CA,
    http://calvaryag.org

[2] Hayford, Dr. Jack, *Keys To Revelation*, Jack Hayford Ministries, 14800 Sherman Way, Van
    Nuys, CA 91405, *www.jackhayford.org*

[3] Graham, Billy, Billy Graham Ministries, Tribune Media Services,
    http://www.kansascity.com/2011/11/14/3266145/billy-graham-we-should-not-try.html

[4] Fairchild, Mary, *"The Rapture and the Second Coming of Christ-Is There a Difference?"*
    http://christianity.about.com/od/endtimestopicalstudy/f/secondcomingof.htm

Chapter 8, Appendix I
Revelation and the Rapture

Introduction: Jesus promised and taught of His end-times *return* and of a *gathering* of His own unto Himself at history's conclusion. (Rev. 7:9-17)

At the Last Supper:
> Jesus promised, *"I will come again:* (John 14:3) *and receive you unto myself; that where I am you may be also."*

At His trial:
> *"Tell us if you are the Christ."*
> Jesus answered: *"It is as you said, ...you will see the Son of Man sitting at the right hand of the Power and coming on the clouds of heaven."*
>   (Matt. 26:63-65)

At His ascension into Heaven:
> The angels said*: "Men of Galilee, why do you stand gazing up into heaven? This same Jesus, who was taken up from you into heaven, will so come in like manner as you saw Him go into heaven."*   (Acts 1:11)

Opening Book and last book of Revelation:
> *"Behold, He is coming with clouds, and every eye will see Him...all the tribes of the earth will mourn because of Him."*   (Rev. 1:7)
> *He who testifies to these things says, "Surely I am coming quickly."*
> *Amen. Even so, come, Lord Jesus!*   (Rev. 22:20)

Let's look at the rapture in Revelation.

A. The Bible and the Rapture

1. The word **rapture** in Greek is **harpadzo** and appears 13 times in NT.
    a. **harpadzo** means *to seize, with a sudden, overwhelming force.*
(John 10:12)	Jesus describes a wolf taking the sheep.
(John 10: 28-29)	Jesus says *"no man plucks"* from my hand.
(John 6:15)	The crowd seeks to take Jesus and force Him to become king after Jesus fed the 5000.

    b. *to transport to another setting.*
(Acts 8:39)	As Philip is *"caught away"* by the Spirit, from the desert encounter with Ethiopian, *"found at Azotus, preaching."*

    c. *to seize and rescue from imminent peril.*
(Acts 23:10)	As Apostle Paul is about to be literally torn or "pulled to pieces" by an angry mob in Jerusalem.
(Jude 23)	describing the spirit of compassion motivating our evangelism: "pulling them (KJV—"snatch") as brands..."

2. The definition of the time of the Rapture.
   a. This will occur in conjunction with "the last trumpet"
     (1 Cor. 15:51-52)   *"...for the trumpet shall sound and the dead will be raised...we (the living) shall be changed."*
     (1 Thess. 4:17)   *"...we shall be caught up together..." at the coming of the Lord, when "the Lord Himself will descend from heaven with a shout, with the trumpet of God..."*
   b. This will occur in conjunction with the climax of age-long struggle/travail of humanity that Jesus calls the *"great tribulation."*
     (Matt. 24:29-31)   *"Immediately after..."* (see Matt. 24:1-22)
     The same text reveals a time of cataclysmic consummation on earth: *"sun/moon/stars"*
     —compare with Rev. 6:12-13
     I looked when He opened the sixth seal, and behold there was a great earthquake; and the sun became black as sackcloth of hair, and the moon became like blood. And the stars of heaven fell to the earth, as a fig tree drops its late figs when it is shaken by a mighty wind.

B. The Rapture Texts of Revelation
   1. The text at hand— Rev. 7:9-17. Basic facts about the throng—
     a. There are people *"of all nations*, etc." celebrating a victory (palm leaves, v. 9) and shouting triumphantly v. 10.
     b. They have suddenly arrived, and prompt praise, v. 11, 12.
     c. They have just come out of "the great tribulation" v. 13, 14.
     d. Though this passage presents the basics related to *"raptured host,"* there are other "prophetic view points" of this event in this book.

   2. Three other Revelation perspectives on the rapture—
     a. Rev. 11:11-13, as the Two Witnesses are called "up."
     b. Rev. 14:1-5, as the 144,000 (earlier "sealed") arrive.

     c. These two entities seem to many to be the most difficult to identify in Revelation, because they both relate to the "mystery" role (Rev. 10:7) of the combined witness of believing Jews and Gentiles—a joint, anointed testimony that has continued since the Church's birth, and will till the end.
     d. Rev. 19:1-9, as the joyous redeemed celebrate the Great Supper (v. 9—see Mt. 25:1-13; 22:1-14; Lk. 14:15-24).

C. Rapture Truth and Your Life Today
   1. The promise of being *"caught up together"* is only available to those who have *"washed their robes in His Blood"*   (Rev. 7:14)

   2. There is an <u>ultimate promise of great deliverance</u>.
     "...the ones who come out of the great tribulation"   (Rev. 7:14)

   3. <u>The moment of deliverance</u> will be related to the moment that the Earth Quake occurs.

"...in your patience, possess your souls"   (Luke 21:19)
Read 1 Thessalonians 5:1-11. We are not appointed to wrath (1 Thessalonians 5: 9), but we are called to sobriety (1 Thessalonians 5: 6- 7) and sensitive preparedness   (1 Thessalonians 5: 8).

4. <u>There will be great relief</u> from distress and great comfort from pain and heartbreak, as great reward awaits us   (Rev. 22: 12)

Conclusion
- Who will notice "the rapture" has occurred?
- The awesome likelihood is that no one will, except those who are gone!
- Society's disposition to disbelieve will attribute all to "the cataclysm."

References:
[1] Hayford, Dr. Jack, *Unlocking the End-Book Study Guide*, Living Way Ministries, CA, 1998

Chapter 8, Appendix II
Summary Lessons from the Study of Revelation

A. Jesus Christ is Lord of the Church and is actively present all the while -
1. to receive our worship
2. to evaluate our actions
3. to sustain us in trial
4. and to lead us to overcoming victory.

B. Jesus Christ is Lord of the Earth, and as Creator/Redeemer -
1. has unfolded the "deed" (scroll) to reclaim it
2. has commissioned His own to evangelize it
3. is executing justice and judgment toward its ultimate cleansing and renewal
4. and will ultimately rule it in righteousness

C. God's tireless dealings with Israel as a people -
1. are constant in a personal sense now;
2. are suspended in a national sense until "about now"
3. and will be ultimately realized in a way yet undefined; though partially prophesied.

D. The Adversary, the Devil, is a relentless, age-long foe, who -
1. is manifest in the world system by controlling it
2. is systematic in opposing God by blaspheming all that pertains to Him
3. is merciless in his deployment of demon beings to torment and destroy mankind
4. and is to be ultimately and conclusively judged and consigned to eternal torment.

E. This world is on a certain "path" of deterioration; so that -
1. all its environment is deteriorating as man violates it
2. all its political, economic, and spiritual systems are damned
3. and it will ultimately be disintegrated and replaced by a new creation.

References:
[1] Hayford, Dr. Jack, *Unlocking the End-Book Study Guide*, Living Way Ministries, CA, 1998

Chapter 8, Appendix III
Days of Noah - Prayer of Repentance for America

In January of 1996, the Rev. Joe Wright, senior pastor of the 2,500-member Central Christian Church in Wichita, delivered the following opening "Prayer of Repentance" at a session of the Kansas House of Representatives.

- Heavenly Father, we come before you today to ask your forgiveness and seek your direction and guidance.

- We know your Word says, "Woe to those who call evil good," but that's exactly what we've done.

- We have lost our spiritual equilibrium and inverted our values.

- We confess that we have ridiculed the absolute truth of your Word and called it moral pluralism.

- We have worshipped other gods and called it multiculturalism.

- We have endorsed perversion and called it an alternative lifestyle.

- We have exploited the poor and called it the lottery.

- We have neglected the needy and called it self-preservation.

- We have rewarded laziness and called it welfare.

- We have killed our unborn and called it choice.

- We have shot abortionists and called it justifiable.

- We have neglected to discipline our children and called it building esteem.

- We have abused power and called it political savvy.

- We have coveted our neighbors' possessions and called it ambition.

- We have polluted the air with profanity and pornography and called it freedom of expression.

- We have ridiculed the time-honored values of our forefathers and called it enlightenment.

- Search us O God and know our hearts today; try us and see if there be some wicked way in us; cleanse us from every sin and set us free.

- Guide and bless these men and women who have been sent here by the people of Kansas, and who have been ordained by you, to govern this great state.

- Grant them your wisdom to rule and may their decisions direct us to the center of your will. I ask it in the name of your son, the living savior, Jesus Christ.

    Amen.

Chapter 8, Appendix IV
Predictions and Claims for the Second Coming of Christ

Some examples of individuals or organizations
who tried to predict the time of Jesus' coming.[1]

Predicted dates	Claimant just since 1975	Description
1975	Herbert W. Armstrong	Armstrong, Pastor-General of the Radio Church of God, and then the Worldwide Church of God, felt the return of Jesus Christ might be in 1975. Of particular note was the book *1975 in Prophecy!* written by Armstrong and published by the Radio Church of God in 1956. Though, never explicitly stating a date in the booklet, the title led people to believe the date was the second coming.
1982 Jun 21	Benjamin Creme	Followers of the New Age guru Benjamin Crème believe the Second Coming will occur when Maitreya (whom they identify as being Christ) makes his presence on Earth publicly known. Creme put ads in many major world newspapers in early 1982 that the Second Coming would occur on Monday, 21 June 1982.
1999 to 2009	Jerry Falwell	Fundamentalist preacher who predicted in 1999 that the Second Coming would probably be within 10 years
2000	Ed Dobson	This pastor predicted the end would occur in his book *The End: Why Jesus Could Return by A.D. 2000.*
2000, April 6	James Harmston	The leader of the True and Living Church of Jesus Christ of Saints of the Last Days predicted the Second Coming of Christ would occur on this day.
1994 Sep 6 / 2011 May 21 / 2011 Oct 21	Harold Camping	He served as president since 1958 of a California-based radio station group that broadcasts to more than 150 markets in the United States. Camping claimed Judgment Day would be in 1994. He then said the rapture would be on May 21, 2011 with 5 months of brimstone and plagues on Earth, followed by the destruction of the universe on October 21 of the same year.
2011 Sep 29 / 2012 May 27	Ronald Weinland	Weinland predicted Jesus would return on September 29, 2011. When his prediction failed to come true he moved the date of Jesus return to May 27, 2012.
2012	Jack Van Impe	Televangelist, over the years, predicted many specific years and dates for the second coming of Jesus, but has continued to move his prediction later. Many of these dates have already passed, and he recently pointed to 2012 as a possible date for the second coming. Van Impe no longer claims to know the exact date of the Second Coming, but quotes verses which imply that mankind should know when the second coming is near.

The Jehovah's Witnesses have made many claims over the last one hundred thirty years predicting the Second Coming [2]

Predicted dates	Jehovah's Witnesses Claims
1889	The 'battle of the great day of God Almighty' ... which will end in A.D. 1914 ... is already commenced
1904	The stress of the great time of trouble will be on us soon, somewhere between 1910 and 1912 - culminating ... October 1914
1914	The great crisis, the great clash...is very near. Armageddon may begin next spring
1922	The date 1925 is even more distinctly indicated by the Scriptures than 1914
1923	Our thought is, that 1925 is definitely settled by the Scriptures. The Christian now has much more upon which to base his faith than Noah had upon which to base his faith in a coming deluge.
1925	The year 1925 is here. Many confidently expect that all members of the body of Christ will be changed into heavenly glory during this year
1926	Some anticipated that the work would end in 1925, but the Lord did not state so. The difficulty was that the friends inflated their imaginations beyond reason; and that when their imaginations burst asunder, they were inclined to throw away everything
1930	The great climax is at hand
1941	Armageddon is surely near....soon....within a few years
1946	Armageddon....should come sometime before 1972
1969	Within months, or at the most five years, the end of the world as we have known it will occur and a thousand year reign of Jesus will begin

References:

[1] http://en.wikipedia.org/wiki/Predictions_and_claims_for_the_Second_Coming_of_Christ
[2] http://www.blueletterbible.org/study/cults/exposejw/expose28.pdf

CHAPTER NINE
LESSONS FROM THE SCHOOL OF PRAYER

Lessons from the "School of Prayer" from the Word of God
and from the lives of godly people who are "doers of the Word"

Jesus said to them,
"It is written, 'My house shall be called a house of prayer "
(Matthew 21:13a)

He who comes to God must believe that He is and
that He is a rewarder of those who diligently seek Him.
(Hebrews 11: 6)

A. The School of Prayer [1]

Dr. Bob Willhite is the author of the book "Why Pray?" printed in English, Spanish, Chinese, Korean, and German. This book is highly recommended as an excellent reference on how to pray. Larry Lea has said that we should "Take this godly man's teaching and devour it. The truths Dr. Willhite shares in his book will inspire you to pray as never before!"

Dr. Willhite tells us in "Why Pray?":

*"My parents and the preachers that peppered my childhood set me on a path that I call the **'School of Prayer'**. Older and/or wiser people who prayed taught me many of the lessons I've learned, but **the Holy Spirit has been my major professor**. Throughout my sixty years on earth, I've taken many questions to Him:*

- o *Why did I sometimes pray with what seemed to be much faith-and yet I saw no answer?*
- o *Why, at other times, did I pray with what seemed little faith, and I received an immediate answer?*
- o *Why did God want me to pray?*
- o *Did He not have all power in heaven and in earth?*
- o *If He had a will and all power, why didn't He just do what He willed and had the power to do?"*

1. Knowing that God's Word says, "Seek Me and you shall find Me", Dr. Willhite began to seek God wholeheartedly.

   a. As he sought God, the Lord revealed certain truths to him that he put into his book, "Why Pray?"

   b. Dr. Willhite encourages us in his book saying: *"As you begin to seek God, the Lord will also reveal His truths to you."*

B. Why Don't Christians Pray? [1]

1. Some people have prayed and were disappointed in the outcome of their prayers.

   a. "I prayed and nothing happened"

   b. They began to question God's love and quit praying consistently

2. So, some people don't pray because they are dominated by doubt -

   a. doubt that God exists

   b. or doubt that God can do anything He has committed Himself to do

   c. Most people have self doubt that they cannot pray effectually

3. But we Christians are called to pray. Jesus said:

   "My house shall be called a house of prayer"   (Matt. 21: 13)

4. Today, the temple of God is <u>not</u> a building.

   a. The church meets in a building, but we believers are the temple of the Holy Ghost both corporately and individually

      Do you not know that you are the temple of God and that the Spirit of God dwells in you?

      Or do you not know that your body is the temple of the Holy Spirit who is in you, whom you have from God, and you are not your own?

      (1 Cor. 3: 16; 6: 19)

   b. Paul said that we are being built for a *"dwelling place of God in the Spirit"*

      (Eph. 2:22)

   c. Our hearts will <u>not</u> become a house of prayer until we decide to set ourselves in agreement with heaven on this matter

   d. Ask Him to help you become what He desires- a dwelling place of the Holy Spirit and a house of prayer

C. "Baby" Faith [1]

1. Our Heavenly Father uses things in our lives to teach us important lessons in prayer.

    a. God takes us where we are and patiently teaches us that He loves us and will respond to our prayers- even if those prayers don't seem very important.

    b. Have you ever noticed how new Christians seem to receive an answer to every prayer? They pray, "Lord, I need a parking place near the covered walk; it's raining." And, sure enough, there it is. God gives them a parking place not ten feet from the canopy.

        o   Is this because they had such great faith or because they had such little faith?

        o   It may be because they had such little faith. Our Father takes us right where we are.

        o   He knows our faith is little and that it rests more in what He does than in who He is.

2. Think of this in terms of a baby.

    a. Babies are selfish and self-centered, but babies are expected to grow up at some point in time.

    b. Painful though it is, our heavenly Father God will see to it that we grow.

    c. There will come a time when we will pray about some little matter, and nothing will happen. There will be no answer:

        o   not because we have no faith or have failed God in some way

        o   but because our Father wants us to see beyond ourselves

D. Selflessness Needed [1]

1. Selfishness—concerned excessively or only with ourself— is the natural tendency of the flesh. We will never be totally free from it in this life, but with understanding and the help of the Holy Spirit we can be less selfish.

2. Selflessness— not having any concern for ourself— must be one of the most important goals of our lives. Jesus is our example, and He said to His followers:

    "If anyone desires to come after Me, let him deny himself, and take up his cross, and follow Me"   (Matt. 16:24)

    a. He did not lead His followers to a throne, but He led them to a cross

    b. not to wealth, but to self-denial

      c. <u>not</u> to fame, but to indignity

      d. <u>not</u> to victory, but to what seemed to be defeat

      e. One cannot experience resurrection until there has been a crucifixion of the self-life

3. In Ephesians 4:12-13, Paul reveals that God's intention is the perfecting and the full equipping of the saints

      a. that we might arrive at mature adulthood—the completeness of personality which is nothing less than Christ's own perfection.

      b. This implies spiritual progression—a growth toward maturity.

E. Growing Faith [1]

1. Dr. Willhite's dad was a Christian all of his life and would often testify: "I never got serious with God about anything for which I did not get an answer."

      a. Dr. Willhite's mom was rushed to hospital emergency following a stroke, and a little while later she went to be with her Lord.

      b. His dad was grieved because of her death, but there was another matter that troubled him. He had prayed and God had not responded.

      c. His dad then went through doubt and a challenge to his faith.

2. Faith must have a transition at some point in life.

      a. **Our faith must rest in Whom God is - not in what He does**.

      b. He is God even when it looks like He does not respond to our prayers.

      c. He does not answer every prayer we pray the way we want -

          o not because He does not have the power

          o but because in His judgment, it would not be best to do so

3. Abraham said, *"Shall not the Judge of all the earth do right?"*   (Gen. 18:25)
    a. Abraham meant the question to encourage the listeners to think about the question.
    b. Of course, God will always do the right thing.
    c. Dr. Willhite is thankful that God had not answered all of his prayers.
    d. The world would be in quite a mess if God granted every prayer request.
    e. We are just not smart enough to tell God what to do.

4. Of course we want our way, but if we are wise, we will say with Jesus:

    "Nevertheless not My will, but Yours, be done "   (Luke 22:42)

F. Praying with All Your Heart [1]

1. Jesus prayed-aloud and with emotions:
    *During the days of Jesus' life on earth, **He offered up prayers and petitions with fervent cries and tears** to the one who could save Him from death, and **He was heard because of His reverent submission**.*   (Heb. 5: 7)

2. The Feelings and emotions do touch our Lord.
    The Word of God assures us that our high priest can be *"touched with the feeling of our weaknesses"*   (Heb. 4: 15, KJV)

3. The Old Testament story in 2 Kings 20: 1-6 illustrates this fact very well. God told the prophet Isaiah to tell Hezekiah that the king was going to die. Hezekiah's response was to pray and weep bitterly. God spoke to Isaiah again and said,
    Return and tell Hezekiah ... :
    "I have heard your prayer, I have seen your tears;
    surely I will heal you ... and I will add to your days fifteen years."
    Our Father was moved by Hezekiah's tears - touched by his emotions.

4. Emotions are a vital part of prayer. As James 5: 16 says:
    The effectual fervent prayer of a person in right standing with God releases tremendous power.   (Dr. Willhite's paraphrase)
    a. **effectual** means able to produce a desired effect
    b. **fervent** means exhibiting great intensity of feeling

     c. ***effectual fervent*** prayer has great intensity of feeling and produces great power

     d. The greater the need, the more intensely we feel it

5. It would <u>not be</u> emotionally or psychologically honest to come before God with a religious prayer such as:

     a. "Thou most high God, Creator of heaven and earth, hear the plea of this Thy humble servant as I calmly communicate with Thee about this emergency."

     b. Dr. Willhite writes: *To be honest, we should lift up our voices with strong crying and tears.*

G. God is Good [1]

1. Dr. Willhite writes that he was always <u>trying to make himself worthy of His blessings</u>, and was <u>always falling short</u>.

     a. One Sunday when he was praying a the church, just waiting on the Lord, drawing near to Him, he prayed, "Lord, I want to ask You to do this one thing for me, but I don't feel worthy…"

     b. The Lord spoke to him saying, "Son, whatever gave you the idea that I bless you because you are good. I bless you because I am good."

     c. The Word from the Lord showed Dr. Willhite that he can come before Him with confidence and pray

       o <u>not</u> at a throne of judgment

       o <u>not</u> with our righteousness from human effort

       o but to pray boldly at *"the throne of grace"*   (Hebrews 4: 16)

       o and to pray with the righteousness God provides by the blood of His Son Jesus to all who will receive it by faith in Him

---

God does not hear your prayers and bless you
because you are good, but **because He is good**.

H. Praying in Jesus' Name [1]

> *"Whatever you **ask in My name**, that I will do,*
> *that the Father may be glorified in the Son.*
> *If you ask anything in My name, I will do it"*   (John 14: 13-14)

1. What a powerful, seemingly all-inclusive verse of Scripture, but the qualifying clause is ***"ask in My name"***

2. Once, Dr. Willhite said *"Lord, I have asked things in Jesus' name and they have <u>not</u> been done.*
   a. *"I had no sooner spoken when the Father said, 'Son, you do not know what it means to ask in Jesus' name.'*
   b. *"I thought about that word, I knew He was right. I know how to ask in Jesus' name. All I was doing was presenting my 'want list' and then saying, 'In Jesus' name, amen.'*
   c. *"It seemed to me that I was using that name without any real understanding of what it meant.*
   d. *"Much prayer and a thorough study revealed that Jesus was in effect saying:*

   > **'Whatever you ask by My command and My authority,**
   > **acting in My behalf, for the advancement of My kingdom,**
   > **I will do, that the Father may be glorified in the Son.' "**

   e. *"To pray in Jesus' name took on a new meaning. Suddenly, the kingdom comes back into focus.*
   f. *Prayer was to be <u>primarily in behalf of His kingdom</u>. I could see it.*
   g. *We have been authorized to act in His behalf for the advancement of His kingdom. "*

I. Why Pray? [1]

1. Why would an omnipotent, omniscient God need us to pray? Can He not do what He wants to do without us? Is there something God lacks that we can contribute to Him, some insufficiency that we can supply trough our prayer?

2. This example helps illustrate one way we are commanded to pray.

   But when He (Jesus) saw the multitudes, He was moved with compassion for them, because they were weary and scattered, like sheep having no shepherd. Then He said to His disciples, "The harvest truly is plentiful, but the laborers are few. Therefore pray the Lord of the harvest to send out laborers into His harvest' "   (Matthew 9:36-38)

   a. Jesus saw the multitudes and was moved with compassion. Thank God, we have a Savior who has emotions. He felt something when He saw people as sheep having no one to lead them. They were lost, with no sense of direction. Many are lost and do not even know it.

   b. We agree we have to do something about bringing in the harvest. But pray?
      o That is what Jesus said to do. Yes, pray! Pray! Pray!
      o We have done about everything except pray, although we do a little of that also: "Lord, now bless our best efforts, we pray, in Jesus' name. Amen."
      o All of the above things may be all right, but they are not what Jesus instructed us to do. Perhaps some are saying: I know what Jesus said to do, but it doesn't make good sense.

   c. Why do we need to pray about something that is so obviously His will?
      o It is His harvest. His followers are His laborers.
      o If He wants them sent, why doesn't He just send them?

3. Dr. Willhite agrees that it doesn't make sense—unless you understand how God implements His will.

   a. Two hundred years ago John Wesley said, "God does nothing but in answer to prayer."

   b. God must wait until He is asked, before He can do what He wants to do— not because He is powerless, but because of the way He has chosen to exercise His will.

   c. Jesus was saying, "I want to send laborers, but you must pray. When you pray, I will send the laborers." God will do these things, but not until He is asked.

   d. The same principle is found in James:

      "You do not have because you do not ask"   (James 4:2)

4. We must pray; it is the only way God can legally intervene. Dr. Willhite writes:

   a. *What I tried to show in this teaching is that God operates by divine law and established principle; He exercises His will under strict rules.*

   b. *He has chosen to involve us in that process. And to me, that is exciting.*

   c. *We are not pawns on some great chessboard of life to be moved about by forces over which we have no control. We are involved.*

   d. *We are working together with God in the implementation of His holy will.*

   e. *Get these truths in your spirit and your attitude toward life will change. You can make a difference; you can set up the conditions under which things can be changed.*

J. Foundational Principles for Prayer [2]

1. God desires to communicate with us.

2. Prayer is rooted in a personal relationship with God.
   Its purpose is to strengthen and deepen your intimacy with Him.

3. The ultimate conversation is not just about you talking to God.
   To truly interact with Him, you must listen to Him as well.

References:

[1] Willhite, Dr. Bob. *Why Pray?*, Creation House, 1982

[2] Stanley, Dr. Charles F., *The Ultimate Conversation, Talking with God through Prayer*, In Touch Ministries, Inc., 2012

Chapter 9, Appendix I
Example of Daily Prayer Alert from July 25, 2013

The page shown below is from the "National Call to Prayer" daily prayer website that Dr. Bob Willhite posts on the internet every Monday-Friday. To sign up for the Daily Prayer Alert to be emailed to you, go to *http://nationalcalltoprayer.org/* and then follow the instructions on the right side of the page that says *"Sign up to receive the weekday prayer alert to your email!"*

Ladies and Gentlemen, we know that the Lord our God HEARS our prayers!

Now this is the confidence that we have in Him, that if we ask anything according to His will, He hears us. And if we know that He hears us, whatever we ask, we know that we have the petitions that we have asked of Him.   (1John 5:14-15)

Dear Lord,

If tomorrow never comes on this earth, I pray that I will leave behind a testimony that points to YOU. Help me to live as if today were my last before entering Eternity, for I know not what the day may bring. I pray that I will love others with a Godly LOVE.

I PRAY that I will be kind and considerate, that I will share exactly who YOU are and what YOU have done. I will smile at those I see throughout the day, that I will remember and pray for others as You Jesus, have prayed for me. I will appreciate every little thing and have an attitude of gratitude, that I will be honest and responsible in all things.

THANK YOU LORD for Blessing me and loving me and filling me with Your Spirit. Please feed my soul and give me strength this day. May YOU always be Glorified and my family be Blessed in our rising up and our laying down. May I touch lives and sow seeds of Your Word throughout the day. In the Name of Your Son my Savior I pray,

Amen and Amen!

Chapter 9, Appendix II
Talking to the Father through Prayer [1]

Prayer is life's greatest time-saver and is always our most productive course of action

1. When emergencies arise, we can receive clear, timely direction from the Lord through prayer, which eliminates confusion.

2. As we converse with the Father, He can keep us from making wrong decisions that would have negative, long-range repercussions or would cause costly delays.

3. Through intimate communion with the Savior, worry, anxiety, and fretting can be eliminated because we grow in our assurance of His character.

4. Even if we should start down the wrong path out of ignorance, God can get us back on track as we spend time in His presence and listen to Him.

5. Our growing relationships with the Father produce a sense of peacefulness because we enjoy His perfect understanding of our circumstances and His unfailing guidance.

6. Prayer invites the Lord into our daily activities, allowing Him to make us productive.

7. Listening to God gives us confidence and can make our decisions more enjoyable because we're doing what He's called us to do.

8. Time with the Savior sharpens our discernment, helping us avoid wasted opportunities.

9. We receive the Lord's viewpoint regarding our situations, seeing through surface issues to what's really happening.

10. Our communion with the Father gives us energy, enabling us to accomplish the great things He calls us to do.

11. Focusing on the Lord prevents us from being distracted by the wrong things.

12. The Holy Spirit reminds us of the necessity to act upon important decisions and activities that we may forget or wrongly consider insignificant.

13. Abiding in God's presence prevents us from becoming discouraged because He always fills us with hope.

14. Remaining constant in our communication with the Father reveals open doors of opportunity that we would not have seen otherwise.

15. Committing our ways to the Lord through prayer helps us discern the difference between busyness and true fruitfulness.

References:

[1] Stanley, Dr. Charles F., *From the Pastor's Heart*, In Touch Ministries, Inc., October 2012

Chapter 9, Appendix III
Jesus Prayed Continually and Taught about Prayer

The scriptures below show several examples of Jesus praying and several examples of Jesus teaching about prayer and how to pray.

1. **Jesus prays for the little children and blesses them**
   *Then little children were brought to Him **that He might put His hands on them and pray**, but the disciples rebuked them.*   (Matthew 19:13)

2. **Jesus' Prayer in the Garden**
   *Then Jesus came with them to a place called Gethsemane, and said to the disciples, "Sit here **while I go and pray** over there."*
   *He went a little farther and fell on His face, and **prayed**, saying, "O My Father, if it is possible, let this cup pass from Me; nevertheless, not as I will, but as You will."*
                              (Matthew 26:36, 42, 44; Mark 14:32, 35, 38; Luke 22:39-46)

3. **Jesus prayed while John baptized Him**
   When all the people were baptized, it came to pass that Jesus also was baptized; and while He prayed, the heaven was opened.   (Luke 3:21)

4. **Jesus prayed just before Peter confesses Him as the Son of the Living God**
   *And it happened, as **He was alone praying**, that His disciples joined Him, and He asked them, saying, "Who do the crowds say that I am?"*   (Luke 9:18)

5. **Jesus prays at His transfiguration on the Mount**
   *Now it came to pass, about eight days after these sayings, that He took Peter, John, and James and **went up on the mountain to pray**. As He prayed, the appearance of His face was altered, and His robe became white and glistening.* (Luke 9:28-29)

6. **Jesus prays for Himself**
   Jesus spoke these words, lifted up His eyes to heaven, and said: "Father, the hour has come. Glorify Your Son, that Your Son also may glorify You"   (John 17:1)

7. Jesus prays for His disciples

"I have manifested Your name to the men whom You have given Me out of the world. They were Yours, You gave them to Me, and they have kept Your word."
(John 17:6)

"But I have prayed for you, that your faith should not fail; and when you have returned to Me, strengthen your brethren."   (Luke 22:32)

"I pray for them. I do not pray for the world but for those whom You have given Me, for they are Yours."   (John 17:9)

"I do not pray that You should take them out of the world, but that You should keep them from the evil one."   (John 17:15)

8. Jesus prays for all believers

"I do not pray for these alone, but also for those who will believe in Me through their word"   (John 17:20)

9. Pray for your enemies

"But I say to you, love your enemies, bless those who curse you, do good to those who hate you, and <u>pray for those</u> who spitefully use you and persecute you"
(Matthew 5:44)

"Bless those who curse you, and pray for those who spitefully use you."
(Luke 6:28)

10. Praying to be noticed

"And <u>when you pray</u>, you shall not be like the hypocrites. For they love to pray standing in the synagogues and on the corners of the streets, that they may be seen by men. Assuredly, I say to you, they have their reward.
But you, <u>when you pray</u>, go into your room, and when you have shut your door, pray to your Father who is in the secret place; and your Father who sees in secret will reward you."   (Matthew 6:5)

"…who devour widows' houses, and for a pretense make long prayers. These will receive greater condemnation."   (Luke 20:47)

11. Pray and fast

"However, this kind does not go out except by prayer and fasting."

(Matthew 17:21)

So He said to them, "This kind can come out by nothing but prayer and fasting."

(Mark 9:29)

12. Do not pray with repetition

"And when you pray, do not use vain repetitions as the heathen do. For they think that they will be heard for their many words." (Matthew 6:5-7)

13. Pray in this manner

In this manner, therefore, pray: Our Father in heaven, Hallowed be Your name.

(Matthew 6:9)

14. Pray for laborers

"Therefore pray the Lord of the harvest to send out laborers into His harvest."

(Matthew 9:38)

Then He said to them, "The harvest truly is great, but the laborers are few; therefore pray the Lord of the harvest to send out laborers into His harvest. (Luke 10:2)

15. Jesus solitary prayer

And when He had sent the multitudes away, He went up on the mountain by Himself to pray. Now when evening came, He was alone there. (Matthew 14:23)

16. House of prayer

And He said to them, "It is written, 'My house shall be called a house of prayer,' but you have made it a 'den of thieves.'" (Matthew 21:13)

Then He taught, saying to them, "Is it not written, 'My house shall be called a house of prayer for all nations'? But you have made it a 'den of thieves.' " (Mark 11:17)

Then He went into the temple and began to drive out those who bought and sold in it, saying to them, "It is written, 'My house is a house of prayer,' but you have made it a 'den of thieves.'" (Luke 19:45-46)

17. Pray believing

And whatever things you ask in prayer, believing, you will receive." (Matthew 21:22)

18. Prayer to His Father

Or do you think that I cannot now pray to My Father, and He will provide Me with more than twelve legions of angels?   (Matthew 26:53)

19. Jesus solitary prayer

Now in the morning, having risen a long while before daylight, He went out and departed to a solitary place; and there He prayed   (Mark 1:35)
And when He had sent them away, He departed to the mountain to pray.
                                                                                                (Mark 6:46)
Now it came to pass in those days that He went out to the mountain to pray, and continued all night in prayer to God.   (Luke 6:12)
So He Himself often withdrew into the wilderness and prayed.   (Luke 5:16)

20. Prayer and forgiveness

Therefore I say to you, whatever things you ask when you pray, believe that you receive them, and you will have them.
And whenever you stand praying, if you have anything against anyone, forgive him, that your Father in heaven may also forgive you your trespasses.   (Mark 11:24-25)

21. Watch and pray

Take heed, watch and pray; for you do not know when the time is.   (Mark 13:33)

22. Prayer of John the Baptist's father

But the angel said to him, "Do not be afraid, Zacharias, for your prayer is heard; and your wife Elizabeth will bear you a son, and you shall call his name John.
                                                                                                (Luke 1:13)

23. The Model Prayer

Now it came to pass, as He was praying in a certain place, when He ceased, that one of His disciples said to Him, "Lord, teach us to pray, as John also taught his disciples."
So He said to them, "When you pray, say: Our Father in heaven, Hallowed be Your name. Your kingdom come. Your will be done On earth as it is in heaven.
                                                                                                (Luke 11:1-2)

24. Pray always

Men always ought to pray and not lose heart,   (Luke 18:1)

25. Prayer of the Pharisee and the Tax collector

"Two men went up to the temple to pray, one a Pharisee and the other a tax collector.

The Pharisee stood and prayed thus with himself, 'God, I thank You that I am not like other men—extortioners, unjust, adulterers, or even as this tax collector.
                    (Luke 18:10-11)

26. Pray to escape Tribulation

Watch therefore, and pray always that you may be counted worthy to escape all these things that will come to pass, and to stand before the Son of Man."
                    (Luke 21:36)

27. Jesus prayed for His Father to send the Holy Spirit

And I will pray the Father, and He will give you another Helper, that He may abide with you forever.   (John 14:16)

28. Jesus said to ask in His Name

In that day you will ask in My name, and I do not say to you that I shall pray the Father for you.   (John 16:26)

29. The Disciples prayed after Jesus ascended to heaven

And when they had entered, they went up into the upper room where they were staying: Peter, James, John, and Andrew; Philip and Thomas; Bartholomew and Matthew; James the son of Alphaeus and Simon the Zealot; and Judas the son of James.

These all continued with one accord in prayer and supplication, with the women and Mary the mother of Jesus, and with His brothers.   (Acts 1:13-14)

CHAPTER TEN
STEWARDSHIP IS FAITH'S RESPONSE TO GOD

He who is faithful in what is least is faithful also in much;
and he who is unjust in what is least is unjust also in much.
Therefore if you have not been faithful in the unrighteous mammon,
who will commit to your trust the true riches?
And if you have not been faithful in what is another man's,
who will give you what is your own?
(Luke 16: 10-12)

A. Introduction to Stewardship

1. When you hear someone say they are going to talk about stewardship, what things come to your mind?

2. What is a steward?

3. What does a steward do?

4. Jesus gives some tests of a steward in Luke 16.
   A good steward is faithful, owes nothing, but manages everything.

   He who is faithful in what is least is faithful also in much;
   and he who is unjust in what is least is unjust also in much.
   Therefore if you have not been faithful in the unrighteous mammon,
   who will commit to your trust the true riches?
   And if you have not been faithful in what is another man's,
   who will give you what is your own?   (Luke 16:10-12)

B. Six Biblical Principles of Stewardship

1. God owns everything.

   "The land shall not be sold permanently, for the land is Mine; for you are strangers and sojourners with Me."   (Leviticus 25:23)

For every beast of the forest is Mine, And the cattle on a thousand hills.
I know all the birds of the mountains, And the wild beasts of the field are Mine.
If I were hungry, I would not tell you; For the world is Mine, and all its
fullness.   (Psalm 50:10-12)

Indeed heaven and the highest heavens belong to the LORD your God, also the
earth with all that is in it.   (Deuteronomy 10:14)

Yours, O Lord, is the greatness, the power and the glory,
the victory and the majesty; For all that is in heaven and in earth is Yours;
Yours is the kingdom, O LORD, and You are exalted as head over all.
Both riches and honor come from You, and You reign over all.
In Your hand is power and might; In Your hand it is to make great
and to give strength to all.   (1 Chronicles 29:11-12)

The earth is the LORD's, and all its fullness,
The world and those who dwell therein.   (Psalm 24:1)

For if we live, we live to the Lord; and if we die, we die to the Lord. Therefore,
whether we live or die, we are the Lord's.   (Romans 14:8)

2. God has entrusted what He owns to us.

Then God blessed them, and God said to them, "Be fruitful and multiply; fill
the earth and subdue it; have dominion over the fish of the sea, over the birds
of the air, and over every living thing that moves on the earth."
And God said, "See, I have given you every herb that yields seed which is on
the face of all the earth, and every tree whose fruit yields seed; to you it shall
be for food.   (Genesis 1:28-29)

Moreover it is required in stewards that one be found faithful.

                                                                    (1 Corinthians 4:2)

Command those who are rich in this present age not to be haughty, nor to trust in uncertain riches but in the living God, who gives us richly all things to enjoy. Let them do good, that they be rich in good works, ready to give, willing to share, storing up for themselves a good foundation for the time to come, that they may lay hold on eternal life.
O Timothy! Guard what was committed to your trust, avoiding the profane and *idle babblings and contradictions of what is falsely called knowledge—*
by professing it some have strayed concerning the faith.
Grace be with you. Amen.   (1 Timothy 6:17-21)

But he who did not know, yet committed things deserving of stripes, shall be beaten with few. For everyone to whom much is given, from him much will be required; and to whom much has been committed, of him they will ask the more.   (Luke 12:48)

3. Possessions compete with the Lord for first place in our lives.
    a. Read this verse from Luke 16 when Jesus said:
        "No servant can serve two masters; for either he will hate the one and love the other, or else he will be loyal to the one and despise the other.
        You cannot serve God and mammon."   (Luke 16:13)

        1) What do you think Jesus means by this statement?
        2) How do we "serve" money?
        3) How does "serving money" keep us from "serving God"?

    b. According to these verses, what do we tend to look to money/possessions for?

    Then one from the crowd said to Him,
    "Teacher, tell my brother to divide the inheritance with me."
    But He said to him, "Man, who made Me a judge or an arbitrator over you?"
    And He said to them, "Take heed and beware of covetousness, for one's life does not consist in the abundance of the things he possesses."
                                                                    (Luke 12:13-15)

Then He spoke a parable to them, saying:
"The ground of a certain rich man yielded plentifully. And he thought within
himself, saying, 'What shall I do, since I have no room to store my crops?'
So he said, 'I will do this: I will pull down my barns and build greater, and
there I will store all my crops and my goods.
And I will say to my soul, "Soul, you have many goods laid up for many years;
take your ease; eat, drink, and be merry."'
But God said to him, 'Fool! This night your soul will be required of you; then
whose will those things be which you have provided?'
"So is he who lays up treasure for himself, and is not rich toward God."

(Luke 12:16-21)

1) Luke 12:13-15   Instead of looking to God, we look to money for significance; for acknowledgement.

2) Luke 12:16-21   Instead of looking to God, we look to money for security.

4. God instructs us to tithe.

   a. Read the following verses from Malachi:

   "For I am the LORD, I do not change;
   Therefore you are not consumed, O sons of Jacob.
   Yet from the days of your fathers
   You have gone away from My ordinances and have not kept them.
   Return to Me, and I will return to you," Says the LORD of hosts.
   "But you said, 'In what way shall we return?'
   "Will a man rob God? Yet you have robbed Me!

   But you say, 'In what way have we robbed You?'
   In tithes and offerings.
   You are cursed with a curse, for you have robbed Me, even this whole nation.
   Bring all the tithes into the storehouse, that there may be food in My house,
   *and **try Me now in this**," says the LORD of hosts,*
   "If I will not open for you the windows of heaven And pour out for you such
   blessing that there will not be room enough to receive it.

"And I will rebuke the devourer for your sakes,
So that he will not destroy the fruit of your ground,
Nor shall the vine fail to bear fruit for you in the field,"
*   says the LORD of hosts;*
"And all nations will call you blessed, For you will be a delightful land,"
says the LORD of hosts.   (Malachi 3:6-12)

    1) What is a tithe?   *10%*
    2) What is God's House?   *The church where God has placed us.*

   b. Read the following verse from Proverbs 3:

Honor the LORD with your possessions, And with the first fruits of all your
increase; So your barns will be filled with plenty, And your vats will overflow
with new wine.   (Proverbs 3:9-10)

    When we tithe, we honor the Lord, and He blesses us.

5. Our motivation in everything we do should be love.

   a. It begins with love; ends with giving. We cannot love without giving.

Let all that you do be done with love.   (1 Corinthians 16:14)

"Do not lay up for yourselves treasures on earth,
where moth and rust destroy and where thieves break in and steal;
but lay up for yourselves treasures in heaven, where neither moth nor rust
destroys and where thieves do not break in and steal."   (Matthew 6:19-20)

But this I say: He who sows sparingly will also reap sparingly,
and he who sows bountifully will also reap bountifully.
So let each one give as he purposes in his heart, not grudgingly or of necessity;
for God loves a cheerful giver.
And God is able to make all grace abound toward you,
that you, always having all sufficiency in all things,
may have an abundance for every good work.   (2 Corinthians 9:6-8)

For God so loved the world that He gave His only begotten Son, that whoever believes in Him should not perish but have everlasting life.
For God did not send His Son into the world to condemn the world, but that the world through Him might be saved.   (John 3:16-17)

6. Offerings are gifts we give to the Lord above our tithe.
   a. Offerings can be sowed in any kind of Ministry: Missionaries, benevolence, building fund, etc.

Stewardship is the responsible management of resources:

- o not the purse, but the person
- o not the money, but the heart
- o not the money, but the Master

References:

[1] *Capstone Church,* Class on Stewardship, *www.thecapstone.org*

Chapter 10, Appendix I
Stewardship- Ownership and Accountability

1. **Some Bible verses can help teach us how to be good stewards over what God has entrusted to us:**
   a. warnings against being in debt (Proverbs 22:7)
   b. importance of saving for the future (Proverbs 21:20)
   c. how God feels about our giving to help others (2 Corinthians 9:6-15)

2. **The main thing that keeps us from living as good stewards is not because we don't understand what needs to be done.**
   a. We do know what needs to be done from verses like those above. But we don't do it. We don't execute the game plan.
   b. Why not? Because the game plan requires us to master our old natures
      - the nature that wants what it wants
      - that puts self-gratification at the center of the decision-making process
      - that hates sacrifice
   c. That's why we fall short, isn't it? Most Christians who are in debt are there because they spend too much on their wants.

3. **We Christians, like everyone else, have a tendency to "gratify the desires of the sinful nature."**
   The things we spend money on are not necessarily sinful in themselves, but they can cause us to:
   a. fail to pay what we owe to our creditors
   b. not be faithful toward the Lord in our giving
   c. fail to give to help others in Christ's name
   d. fail to set aside money for an emergency
   e. fail to save for the future

   The *impulse* to spend on our wants instead of what we should comes from a drive to satisfy our fleshly desires. That drive, unfortunately, is often stronger than our desire to obey God and please Him with our stewardship.

4. We need to take control of our appetites, or inevitably our appetites take control of us.

    a. How do we do this? We can't.

    b. But God's Holy Spirit, who lives within every Christian, can. He is the one who strengthens and empowers.

    c. When we put ourselves under His direction and control, He builds the fruit of His life (one of which is self-control) into us Galatians 5:22-23).

    d. If we will ask Him, if we will let Him, He is the one who can make us the kind of people He wants us to be ... will make us as good as we wish we could be.

    e. That's why Paul says, "Live by the Spirit!" It's the indispensable stewardship verse, the one that makes following all the other stewardship passages possible.

> *I say then: Walk in the Spirit, and you shall not fulfill the lust of the flesh.*
>
> (Galatians 5:16)

Or as the Amplified Bible puts it:

> *But I say, walk* and *live [habitually] in the [Holy] Spirit [responsive to* and *controlled* and *guided by the Spirit]; then you will certainly not gratify the cravings* and *desires of the flesh (of human nature without God).*

References:

[1] Stanley, Dr. Charles F., *Stewardship Galatians 5: Indispensable Advice,* In Touch with Charles Stanley, 2009

Chapter 10, Appendix II
Financial Stewardship

1. **What is Financial Stewardship?**

   a. The Bible uses the term steward many times to explain your relationship to the responsibilities God has given you.

   b. In biblical times a steward was a manager or overseer of another man's money or possessions.

   c. Jesus applied this term to all His followers with the encouragement that they be wise in all their decision-making (Luke 12:40-48).

   d. Paul described himself and all believers as being entrusted with the Gospel, which implies the responsibility to proclaim this message to the world (1 Thess. 2:4) (1 Cor. 9:17).

   e. The elders of the church were also called stewards of the church and responsible to lead and guide the flock of God (Titus 1:7).

2. **Every Christian has been entrusted with the gifts of the Spirit to fulfill the work God has called him (or her) to perform. We are all stewards in one way or another.**

   a. If you work for someone on a job, then you are a steward over the specific responsibility you've been given to perform. If you have employees you are a steward over them.

   b. If you have children, you will have the stewardship over the lives and care of children.

   c. The most important thing for you to remember about your responsibility as a steward, is that you will one day be called to give account for your stewardship (Luke 16:1-2)

   d. The primary issue on that day will be how faithful you've been to whatever stewardship God has given you (Luke 16:10).

   e. Therefore, faithful financial stewardship is one aspect of your relationship that must be understood as fundamental to the success of your marriage and family as a whole.

3. Is Good Financial Stewardship Important for a Marriage?

a. Many problems result in marriage from the failure of one or both partners being responsible with their money.

b. Couples overspend, get into debt, fail to do basic accounting and bank statement reconciliation, don't communicate with each other before making a large purchase, which results in a failure to meet their obligations, which only adds stress to the relationship and disharmony in the home.

c. Many a divorce has occurred as a result of poor financial stewardship. Therefore, these sinful behaviors must stop in your family.

d. In addition, you have the added potential problem of your heart becoming divided over money. Even though money is morally neutral, it is extremely powerful and can easily divide your heart.

e. A divided heart will bring innumerable problems to your life and marriage. Jesus warned His disciples, *"No one can serve two masters; for either he will hate the one and love the other, or else he will be loyal to the one and despise the other. You cannot serve God and mammon"* (Matt. 6:24).

f. David also warned, *"If riches increase, do not set your heart on them"* (Psalm 62:10). Allowing your heart to become divided and becoming set upon riches is a real possibility for any individual or married couple or these warnings would not be found in Scripture.

g. Therefore, you must learn how to be faithful with your finances and keep money as your servant, not your master.

4. One way to be a good steward with your money is to understand the places you must use your money.

a. Fixed bills- fixed monthly and annual bills that must be paid on time for the family to function (Mortgage or rent, utilities, taxes, and insurance (Matt. 17:24, Acts 21:24, Rom. 13:6-7).

b. Other debts- These debts must also be paid on time to be a faithful steward. "The wicked borrows and does not repay, but the righteous shows mercy and gives" (Ps. 37:21). Wisdom would tell you that, for the righteous to be merciful and giving, they must stay out of debt as much as possible so that they may have the resources to give to those in need.

c. Giving- Faithful stewardship also entails giving. There are three types of giving described in Scripture- tithe, offering, and almsgiving.

1) Tithe- the first 10 % of all your increase and is to be given to the Lord. The Jews brought their tithe to the temple, which allowed the temple to operate (Mal. 3:10). A tithe was first seen being given by Abraham, a man of faith, long before the Law was ever instituted (Gen. 14:20). In addition, Jesus also encouraged the tithe not to be left undone (Matt. 23:23).

2) Offering- describes any giving above your tithe, which could be given to the Lord or to the Lord's work, such as to a missionary or to an individual for any reason to bless them (Luke 21:4). Under the Law an offering was called the whole burnt offering. Paul saw a difference between an offering and an almsgiving (Acts 24:17).

3) Almsgiving- a special kind of offering given specifically to the poor (1 Cor. 16:1-4; 2 Cor. 8:1-9:15). Giving in any of these ways must be done remembering that God will never be your debtor, He will always give back to you, *"pressed down, shaken together, and running over"* (Luke 6:38).

d. Savings- Joseph is the best biblical example of a wise man and a good steward who was specifically directed by God to save.

1) Joseph delivered himself and at least two nations from starvation because he obeyed the specific direction to save the grain from the prosperous years of their harvest.

2) Solomon encouraged savings so that we might be able to leave an inheritance to our children and grand-children. *"A good man leaves an inheritance to his children's children, but the wealth of the sinner is stored up for the righteous"* (Prov. 13:22).

e. Discretionary spending- means that some spending is optional and not required.

1) It's the extra money that you possess and choose to spend on things for your needs or enjoyment.

2) Note that Paul even acknowledged this aspect of money when he exhorted those who were rich and who would have plenty of money for discretionary spending.

> *"Command those who are rich in this present age not to be haughty, nor to trust in uncertain riches but in the living God, who gives us richly all things to enjoy. Let them do good, that they be rich in good works, ready to give, willing to share"*   (1 Tim. 6:17-18)

3) Therefore, there is nothing wrong with richly enjoying what God has given you, but be sure you are also rich in good works through your giving.

References:

[1] Carr, Pastor Steve, *Discipleship Series*, Calvary Chapel, Arroyo Grande, CA, *http://calvaryag.org*

Index

Chapter Subheadings and Appendices

Chapter	Title	Page

1 - The Bible is the Word of the Living God.. 11

    A.   God has revealed Himself to us in His Bible..11

    B.   The Old Testament is the revelation of God to man............................ 11

    C.   The New Testament is the revelation of God in His Son..................... 11

    D.   What the Bible is not.. 12

    E.   The Bible's author is God... 12

    F.   The Bible is a collection of 66 books... 12

    G.   Old and New Testaments are referred to as the "Word of God".............. 13

    H.   Jesus Christ and His apostles assure that Scripture is from God............14

    I.   the words in the Bible not been changed over the centuries?................. 14

    J.   Canonization of Scripture 15

    K.   The whole Bible, O.T. and N.T. is from God 16

    L.   How do I start reading the Bible? 17

    M.   How deeply the Lord desires fellowship with us 18

    Appendix I - The New Testament Timeline 19

    Appendix II - Dates Old Testament written and who wrote it? 24

2 - God is the Creator and Sustainer of Everything 27

    A.   God created everything by His Word from nothing 27

    B.   All things were created through Christ Jesus and for Christ Jesus..........27

    C.   We are God's special creation from all He has made 28

    D.   Let us praise God as the Creator 30

    E.   God as Creator or evolution as our god? 30

    F.   Creation and the theory of evolution- Science of each 31

    Appendix I - Evidence to Reject Evolution 33

    Appendix II - Institute for Creation Research 36

    Appendix III - The Creation Evidence Museum 37

Chapter   Title   Page

3 - God the Father, the Son, and the Holy Spirit 38

    A.   the Father, Son, and Holy Spirit together are one and only one God 38

    B.   The Bible shows the one God is a Trinity of Persons 39

    C.   New Testament shows the glorious truth of the Triune God 40

    D.   New Testament clearly distinguishes three Persons 41

    E.   God the Father 41

    F.   God the Son 42

    G.   God the Holy Spirit 44

    H.   The importance of a correct understanding of God's nature 45

    Appendix I - Scriptures about the Triune God 46

    Appendix II - Ways cults attack the Biblical teaching of the Trinity 52

4 - Jesus is Savior, Lord, and Christ 54

    A.   "Christ" means "Messiah" which means "the Anointed" 54

    B.   "Jesus" means "Yahweh is salvation" 55

    C.   Jesus Christ Is Lord 58

    Appendix I – 17 Messianic prophecies from Isaiah 53.............................60

    Appendix II - 12 prophecies from Psalm 22 about the crucifixion...................63

    Appendix III - 19 Messianic prophecies from various psalms.........................66

    Appendix IV - The Appearances of the risen Christ Jesus 74

    Appendix V – The Prophet Daniel's vision of the Son of Man (Jesus) 74

5 - The Holy Spirit is sent by Jesus and the Father 75

    A.   Jesus promised He will send us the Holy Spirit 75

    B.   Jesus promised the Father will send us the Holy Spirit 75

    C.   INDWELL – Jesus said to be filled with the Holy Spirit 76

    D.   Being continually filled with the Holy Spirit 77

    E.   EMPOWER – The Holy Spirit empowers us to be Jesus' witness 77

    F.   TEACH – The Holy Spirit teaches us 78

    G.   COMFORT – The Holy Spirit comforts us 78

    H.   GUIDE - The Holy Spirit guides us 79

Chapter	Title	Page

I.   Jesus said to not be afraid to receive the Holy Spirit 79

Appendix I - Fellowship with the Father, the Son, and the Holy Spirit 81

Appendix II - Walking in the Power of the Holy Spirit 83

Appendix III - The Holy Spirit gives Spiritual Understanding 85

Appendix IV - The Work of God the Holy Spirit 86

6 - The Nine Gifts of the Holy Spirit 87

A.   We Can Misunderstand the Gifts of the Holy Spirit 87

B.   Diversities of The Gifts of the Holy Spirit 88

C.   The Manifestation of the Holy Spirit 89

D.   Gifts of Revelation 89

E.   Gifts of Power 91

F.   Gifts of Speaking 92

G.   The Holy Spirit Distributes the Gifts 93

H.   Are the Gifts for Today or Did They Pass Away with the Apostles? 93

Appendix I - The Acts of the Holy Spirit 95

Appendix II – Healings by Jesus in the Gospels 97

Appendix III - Healing and Deliverance in the Book of Acts 98

Appendix IV – God still Heals the Sick and Saves the Lost Today 100

7 - Share the Good News of the Kingdom 101

A.   "The Gospel" literally means "the good news" and is about Jesus 101

B.   The Holy Spirit anointed the Lord Jesus to preach the good news. 101

C.   We are called to share our faith with those who don't know Christ 102

D.   God wants to make us an effective witness for Him 102

E.   We have been called to the ministry of reconciliation 103

F.   We are called to be a light to this world 103

G.   We are to publicly and openly proclaim His praises 103

H.   We are to teach and share good news of Jesus as we go 103

I.   Jesus promised to teach us how to spread the Gospel 104

J.   Jesus' Instructions on How to be a Witness for Him 104

K.   Jesus encouraged us to pray for God to send workers for the Gospel.... 104

Chapter	Title	Page

L.   The Gospel message in America 105

M.   *"He who believes in Me out of his heart will flow rivers of living water"*.... 105

Appendix I - Capstone Church's Mission – "Tell Somebody" 106

8 - Jesus Christ is Coming Again 108

A.   The Importance of the Second Coming of Jesus Christ 108

B.   The Purpose of these Promises in Scripture about His Return 108

C.   The Manner of His Second Coming 108

D.   The Purpose of His Second Coming 109

E.   The Signs That We Should Look For 109

F.   What Happens Just Prior to His Second Coming? 111

G.   Difference between the Rapture and the Second Coming of Christ 112

H.   The Tribulation Period and the Second Coming of Christ 112

I.   Jesus calls us as members of His Living Church, His Body 113

J.   Can anyone predict the time of Jesus' coming? 113

Appendix I – Revelation and the Rapture 115

Appendix II - Summary Lessons from the Study of Revelation 118

9 - Lessons from the School of Prayer 122

A.   The School of Prayer 122

B.   Why Don't Christians Pray? 123

C.   "Baby" Faith 124

D.   Selflessness Needed 124

E.   Growing Faith 125

F.   Praying with All Your Heart 126

G.   God is Good 127

H.   Praying in Jesus' Name 128

I.   Why Pray? 128

J.   Foundational Principles for Prayer 130

Appendix I – "National Call to Prayer" Daily Prayer Alert 131

Appendix II - Talking to the Father through Prayer 133

Appendix III - Jesus Prayed Continually and Taught about Prayer 135

Chapter   Title   Page

10 - Stewardship is Faith's Response to God 140

  A. Introduction 140
  B. Six Biblical Principles of Stewardship 140
    1. God owns everything 140
    2. God has entrusted to us what He owns 141
    3. Possessions compete with the Lord for first place in our lives 142
    4. God instructs us to tithe 143
    5. Our motivation in everything we do should be love 144
    6. Offerings are gifts we give to the Lord above our tithe 145
  Appendix I – Stewardship- Ownership and Accountability 146
    1. Some Bible verses can help teach us how to be good stewards over what God has entrusted to us 146
    2. The main thing that keeps us from living as good stewards is not because we don't understand what needs to be done 146
    3. We Christians, like everyone else, have a tendency to "gratify the desires of the sinful nature." 146
    4. We need to take control of our appetites, or inevitably our appetites take control of us 147
  Appendix II – Financial Stewardship 148
    1. What is Financial Stewardship? 148
    2. Every Christian has been entrusted with the gifts of the Spirit to fulfill the work God has called him (or her) to perform 148
    3. Is Good Financial Stewardship Important for a Marriage? 149
    4. One way to be a good steward with your money is to understand the places you must use your money 149